MW00774302

*Words and Images
that Seep into the Soul*

Words and Images
that Seep into the Soul

James Phillips Noble (signature)

James Phillips Noble

To Clark & Jayce

Two special People

Phil (signature)

RESOURCE *Publications* · Eugene, Oregon

16 JUNE 2013

WORDS AND IMAGES THAT SEEP INTO THE SOUL

Resource Publications
An Imprint of Wipf and Stock Publishers
199 W. 8th Ave., Suite 3
Eugene, OR 97401
www.wipfandstock.com

ISBN 13: 978-1-62032-554-4
Manufactured in the U.S.A.

To Betty Pope (Popesy) Scott Noble

Contents

Contents

Contents

Contents

PART 13—GOD'S WILL / 241

PART 14—MYSTERY / 249

Preface

FLIGHT ATTENDANTS WILL TELL you that there is a line of lights in the floor that will lead you to safety in case the airplane has an emergency landing and fire. I have glanced at them many times as I turned to see the nearest exits and listened to the pre-flight safety talk.

That thin line of lights you might see in the thick smoke inches from your face is a lifeline when you are crawling to safety.

Phil Noble quotes Admiral Richard Byrd when he describes a thin rope he strung on bamboo poles from his shack out 100 yards into the Antarctic snowfield. He says,

"By running my hand over this, blind man fashion, I could feel my way back and forth in the worst weather; and many were the times I did it when the air was so thick with drift that I could not see past the cowling of my windproof, and the line was a thin cord through chaos."

A thin cord through chaos, a row of lights in a smoke-filled aircraft, these are central images for reading this book. Phil refers to Dag Hammarskjöld's saying "Yes" to someone he doesn't name. Thereafter life had meaning. Phil says it is the difference in a person who goes on his own way and one who lives in response to God. When one says "Yes" to God, the lifeline appears. Thin as it is, it is certainly present. Call it faith.

The late John H. Leith, professor of theology at Union Presbyterian Seminary in Richmond, Virginia, once said that when one separates oneself from the church, something very destructive happens. It shows in relationships, first in one's relationship to God, but immediately in the quality of relationships with other people. We grasp for control, but what we need is a lifeline. Going on one's own way can mean simply plodding along, doing what needs to be done to earn money to buy food, clothing and shelter. But when we are touched by the grace and love of God and respond, we are lifted and carried by a joy and passion. Work is a joy.

As you read Phil's book, look for that lifeline. Phil seeks it in his life's conflicts, tragedies and joys, and he expresses it in these poems and "strippings." Phil Noble's faith is a deep belief in a loving father-God. When Phil approaches this loving God in meditation, he approaches the father who loves him and he reaches for that thin lifeline in the midst of his experience on earth.

To help these poems meet with your life experience, it is helpful to know what was going on in Phil's life when he wrote them. Here are key dates and time periods in Phil's life:

When you read his thoughts on "Strippings" and "Chewing," think of Phil's boyhood on a farm at the little town of Learned, Mississippi, in the 1920s. He was born there in August of 1921, just eight years before the stock market crash and the Great Depression.

In spite of the financial difficulties, he attended King College in Bristol, Tennessee, and graduated *cum laude* in 1942 with a BA degree.

From King he went to Columbia Theological Seminary in Decatur Georgia, a graduate school for Presbyterian ministers, and finished with a Bachelor of Divinity degree in 1945. A few months later, in September, 1945, he married the lively and feisty Betty Pope Scott, the daughter of Milton Scott, who owned Scott Mills in Decatur. Betty, a descendent of the founder of Agnes Scott College, graduated from that school and had a life-long, supportive relationship with the college. At Betty's memorial service on August 10, 2012, Elizabeth Kiss, president of Agnes Scott, said that Betty personified Agnes for all the students on campus.

Phil and Betty had three children, Betty Scott, James Phillips, Jr., and Milton Scott.

Phil started his ministry at the McDonough and Timberridge Presbyterian Churches just south of Atlanta, then went to Second Presbyterian Church in Greenville, S.C., for nine years. But the most significant pastoral ministries for Phil came in Anniston, Alabama, and Charleston, S.C. Phil served as pastor of the First Presbyterian church of Anniston from 1956 until 1971 through the very turbulent years of the Civil Rights Movement. There, observing the violence that had taken place in Birmingham, Alabama, Phil became determined that it would not be repeated in Anniston.

When freedom riders came through the South in 1961 integrating public accommodations, their bus was burned in Anniston. (See Phil's book, *Beyond the Burning Bus, the Civil Rights Revolution in a Southern Town*, published by NewSouth Books in 2003). Phil joined with black ministers and other leaders in Anniston to urge the city government to appoint a bi-racial council. In May 1963, the City Commissioners appointed a Bi-racial Human Relations Council. Phil led that council as its chair, endured death threats toward his family and the beatings of black friends, and successfully integrated the Anniston Public Library in 1963. Phil's account in "The Word of the Gospel" captures the power and sacrifice of that era.

As if that trial by fire were not enough, Phil and Betty's younger son Scott contracted leukemia and died on June 13, 1968. Some of Phil's most poignant poems came from this period in Anniston. Phil's poem, "We are Not in Charge," July 10, 1968, was written one month after Scott's death. Notwithstanding any of the Civil Rights turmoil and deep grief, Phil led the Anniston church in building a soaring new sanctuary.

After the loss of Scott, Phil and Betty and their son Phil, Jr. spent a school year at Cambridge, England, for study and recuperation. There Phil bought a white MG-B GT sports car, which he transported to his next pastorate at First (Scots) Presbyterian Church in Charleston, S.C. in 1972. His "wee car," as Phil called it, would appear at First (Scots) any day that Phil did not walk to the church from their house on Gibbs Street.

My wife Marty and I joined Phil and Betty in 1975 when I came to Charleston to be an associate pastor at First (Scots). These were glorious days for Charleston and the church. Charleston was being gentrified, and the grand old historic houses were being renovated to a pristine state. Joseph P. Riley, Jr., became mayor in December, 1975, and began a long, elegant transformation of the historic city. The Spoleto Festival began in 1977 with Gian Carlo Menotti at the artistic helm, and Phil inaugurated an annual Scottish Heritage celebration at First (Scots).

A master at preaching, worship, leading the congregation, building and establishing programs, Phil led the congregation to a thriving witness in the heart of freshly-emerging Charleston. Phil became the mentor of this young pastor, and I learned much about leading a church that I could not learn from books. I thought of Phil as my best friend and advisor, and I learned at the occasion of his retirement in July of 1989 that many other people thought of him as their best friend, too. He is one of those gifted pastors who touch lives in that way.

After leaving First (Scots) in 1982, Phil became executive secretary of the Board of Annuities and Relief of the Presbyterian Church U.S. just before its reunion with the United Presbyterian Church in the U.S.A. in 1983. This was the reunion of the northern and southern streams of the Presbyterian Church, which had split during the Civil War.

Preface

The most significant event to affect Phil and his poetry recently was the death of his beloved wife Betty, who died on August 7, 2012, following a thirteen-year bout with dementia. Phil's poem, "The Ups and Downs of Life," Nov. 28, 2007, was written during her long illness, and his poem, "Missing Light" was written following her death. This is one of the last poems added to this book.

Reading these poems of Phil Noble, I feel planted, secure, that "all's right with the world." I feel freed from anxieties over finances and everyday things. After I read them, I put my head down on the desk like a school kid and felt that the hand of God was on my shoulder. This God said, "Bill, I am your God. You are my child. All of you."

If you want more faith in this Father who loves you, this book can impact your life.

William P. Lancaster, Jr.
October 8, 2012

Acknowledgments

WORDS AND IMAGES THAT *Seep into the Soul* is a bit unusual in that the quotations and the poetry extend over many years. The quotations come from fifty years of my reading. When a passage struck me as being really significant, I would mark it and give it to my good secretary of many years, Mary Catherine White, who would copy it and put it in a file. It is from that rather large file that I selected the quotations included in the book.

The poems or reflections were written over a period of time from the nineteen sixties to the present time. In regard to my writings, Mary Catherine always encouraged me by saying they ought to be published. I am greatly indebted to her.

In the last few years I have dared to let a few friends read a poem now and then. Adelaide and Bill Owens, Hubert Taylor, Keith and Jennie Johnson, Bill and Marty Lancaster, Martha and Burt Vardeman, and Pat Potter were especially encouraging.

Nobody could be more encouraging than my wife Betty Pope (Popesy) Scott Noble, who for sixty-seven years gave me love and support. My daughter, Betty Scott, and my son, Phil, Jr. were always interested in my poems and reflections and encouraged me to keep writing.

Two necessary parts of the publishing process were getting permission from the publishing companies who had the copyrights for the many quotations in my manuscript and having the manuscript copy edited. A student at Columbia Theological Seminary, Shelton Steen, worked at getting the permissions, and I am grateful to him. Rosemary Raynal, writing instructor at Columbia Theological Seminary, copy edited the manuscript. In addition, she did the many things that were necessary to get the manuscript finalized to go to the publishers. I think the book may never have been published if it had not been for her careful and knowledgeable work. To her I am especially grateful.

Numerous people over the years have blessed my life in so many ways.

Acknowledgments

I am grateful to all of them who have contributed to my growth and development. They shaped my life. If there are significant ideas and special insights in the poems that are helpful to the readers, then much of the credit should go to them.

Introduction

THIS BOOK IS COMPOSED of two parts that are entwined together. There are "markings" of words and images that have seeped in varying degrees into my mind, emotions, psyche, and spirit over many years. They have affected my thinking, feeling, beliefs, attitudes, and to some extent, my actions. To say it another way, these are words and images that I have inhaled.

The reflections I have written are what have "seeped out" over the years. Of course what "seeped in" has greatly affected what has "seeped out." But what has "seeped in" has gone through the filter of my own person or being, and therefore what has "seeped out" in the reflections is not the same as what "seeped in."

In the arrangement of the markings and reflections, there has been no effort to relate them by putting a reflection by a particular, or maybe a bit related, marking. They are really quite at random.

This is not a book to be read through as one reads a novel or history book. A reflection or a marking may be read and left in the mind a while to see if anything from it will seep into the deeper being. It is a bit like going to the grocery store and buying a week's supply of food. The whole week's supply is not eaten at one time, but is taken bite by bite and meal by meal. It brings pleasure as it is eaten and nourishment as it is digested. In a similar manner, the markings and reflections are bites or meals that, as they seep in, bring nourishment to the psyche or soul. Like various foods, some are more nourishing than others, and some taste better than others.

The hope is that the reader may find that much of what seeps into the soul will be interesting and beneficial.

Strippings

I grew up on a farm in Mississippi. One of the chores that my brother and I had was milking the cows. The cows and their calves were separated during the day, the cows being in the pasture and the calves in the lot. In the early evening, the cows were brought into the lot, and the calves immediately rushed to their mothers. A rope would be put around the calves' necks as they were feeding from the mother's udder. After a few minutes, the rope would be tied to a fence post, and the cow would be moved back far enough so that the calf could not reach her. Then we would sit on a milking stool and milk the cow, filling our milk pail. When we could get no more milk from the cow we would let the calf go to its mother. As the calf began feeding again, the mother cow would "let down" more milk into her udder. The calf would then be removed from the cow, and we would begin milking again. The milk we would then get was called "the strippings." This was the richest part of the milk, the cream.

From my readings during my long years of Christian ministry, I have collected pieces that have struck me as having most significant meaning. I call these the "strippings" from my reading.

Chewing

Cattle chew their cuds. This means they first swallow their food, and then later bring it up again and chew it some more. They may bring it back more than once. They do this in order for the food to be digested.

This may be a good pattern for the use of this book. If something that is read seems interesting, muse upon it. That is, think or mediate upon what you have read. You may come back to it more than once. In this way you may digest the meaning, and it may become a part of you. Hopefully it will nourish your mind and spirit.

Comment on Reading

> Those who have read of everything are thought to understand everything too; but it is not always so—reading furnishes the mind only with materials of knowledge; it is thinking that makes what is read ours. We are of the ruminating kind, and it is not enough to cram ourselves with a great load of collections; unless we chew them over again, they will not give us strength and nourishment.
>
> —JOHN LOCKE

Part 1

Life

The Stream of Life

The mighty Mississippi River
Begins as a trickle.
From small springs in Minnesota
It flows southward
Ever becoming larger and larger.
Beginning small and quietly,
It grows as it passes over the rocks
And makes turns as it winds
Its way toward the gulf.
Along the way there are rapids
And occasionally falls,
And wide spaces where
It seems not to be moving.
Again it flows in torrents.
Finally it reaches the gulf
Where it merges into the eternal sea.

So with our lives.
We begin a little child
And grow and change
As we become larger
Experiencing times of rapids and falls,
Twists and turns,
And times of stillness and quietness,
But always moving toward
The time when we will
Enter the gulf of eternal life.

OCTOBER 22, 2007

Short Sighted Living

If we live for this life only, for its baubles and bubbles, for its passing pleasures and transient joys, we shall end up bitterly disappointed men and women, and we shall find life hardly worth the price we have to pay to live it . . . Be sure of this: if we live for the things of this world only, we shall live and die grievously frustrated people. Animals may live so, but not creatures fashioned in the image of God.

— FREDERICK WARD KATES

A Sparkling Moment

Now and then there is a sparkling moment.
Times past flash on my memory.
The good times. The special times.
Childhood experiences.
Adolescence and awareness years.
Special people.
Dreams of future years.

Times present. Gratitude for the past.
Gratitude for the present.
Warm and happy experiences.
Loved ones that care.
Friends that are there.

Times to come. Faith that brings hope.
Love that generates security.
Reflections on past mercies
That are a pledge of future grace.

A glimpse of the wholeness of life.
God was there at the beginning.
God is here now.
God will be there at the end.

Thanks be to God for
His love that is from everlasting to everlasting.

FEBRUARY 5, 2006

Human Life and Divine Purpose

If now we could have faith enough to believe that all human life can be filled with divine purpose; that God saves not only the soul, but the whole of human life; that anything which serves to make men healthy, intelligent, happy, and good is a service to the Father of men; that the kingdom of God is not bounded by the church, but includes all human relations— then all professions would be hallowed and receive religious dignity. A man making a shoe or arguing a law case or planting potatoes or teaching school, could feel that this was itself a contribution to the welfare of mankind, and indeed his main contribution to it.

—WALTER RAUSCHENBUSH

Lesson from the Sun's Daily Journey

As the sun rises over the eastern horizon,
We say, "A new day is born."
The sun slowly makes its way across the sky,
And when it sets large and red
Over the western horizon,
We say, "The day is done."
Then comes the night shrouding
Everything in darkness.

When a little baby child is born,
It is the beginning of a new life.
Gradually the child begins
On the journey of life,
Through childhood and teen years
Into young adulthood, middle age,
And then into old age.
Like the sun that disappears
Over the western horizon,
The one who has lived his day on earth
Disappears into the darkness.

But wait!
Look to the eastern horizon!
The sun rises again bringing the light of day.

So when it seems that the light of life is gone
And all is dark and still,
Our faith in the risen Christ
And the creative power of our Father God,
Will let us know that we emerge
From the darkness of death
To arise on another shore
Where the sun never sets.

(Thoughts stirred by Charles H. Schmitz, *Windows Toward God*)
AUGUST 23, 2008

The Great Danger

The greatest danger, that of losing one's own self, may pass off as quietly as if it were nothing; every other loss, that of an arm, a leg, five dollars, a wife, etc., is sure to be noticed.

—SOREN KIERKEGAARD

The great danger facing us all . . . is not that we shall fall into outright viciousness, nor that we shall be terribly unhappy, nor that we shall feel life has no meaning at all; not those things. The danger is that we may fail to perceive life's greatest meaning, fall short of its highest good, miss its deepest and most abiding happiness, be unable to tender the most needed service, be unconscious of life ablaze with the light of the Presence of God, and be content to have it so, that is the danger.
(The danger is) that some day we may wake up and find that always we have been busy with husks and trappings of life and have really missed life itself.

That is what one prays one's friends may be spared, satisfaction with a life that falls short of the best, that has in it no tingle or thrill which comes from a friendship with the Father.

—PHILLIPS BROOKS

Is What I Am Doing Worthwhile?

Blessed is the person who knows that what
   He is doing is worthwhile!
This comes near to the meaning of life.
I do not want to have a growing sense of
   Meaninglessness within.
Sometimes I am called by pleasure—
   Not called just to an experience of pleasure,
   But called to live for what gives me pleasure.
Sometimes I am called by money—
   Not called to do something for a hundred dollars,
   But called to live for the making of money.
Sometimes I am called by selfishness—
   Not called just to explode, "To hell with the World"
   But called to live as if I cared only for myself.
Sometimes I am called by love—
   Not called just to an experience of love,
   But called to live in love with my fellowman.
Sometimes I am called by need—
   Not just to give a dollar for a meal,
   But called to live in response to man's need.
Sometimes I am called by truth—
   Not just called to tell the truth,
   But called to live by and for that which is true.
Sometimes I am called by God and the Devil—
   The devil has a way of seeking to imitate God,
   And at first the voices sound almost alike.
   But when I answer and am shown
   The picture of pleasure, the feel of money,
   The preeminence of self,
   I know whose voice it is—
   But when I answer and am shown
   The love of human kind, the need of one like myself,
   The freedom of truth,
   I know whose voice it is.

Life

When I hear and respond to a certain voice,
I know that what I am doing is not worthwhile.
When I hear and respond to another certain voice,
I know that what I am doing is worthwhile.
Blessed is the man who knows that what
    he is doing is worthwhile.
For this comes near to the meaning of life.

NOVEMBER 23, 1966

Doing Our Best at All Times

To us all comes, at times, the great note of questioning despair that darkens our horizon and paralyzes our effort: "If there really be a God, if eternal justice really rules the world, "we say, "why should life be as it is? Why do some men starve while others feast? Why does virtue often languish in the shadow while vice triumphs in the sunshine? Why does failure so often dog the footsteps of honest effort, while the success that comes from trickery and dishonor is greeted with the world's applause? How is it that the loving father of one family is taken by death, while the worthless encumbrance of another is spared? Why is there so much unnecessary pain, sorrowing and suffering in the world—why, indeed, should there be any?"

Neither philosophy nor religion can give any final satisfactory answer that is capable of logical demonstration, of absolute proof. There is ever, even after the best explanations, a residuum of the unexplained. We must then fall back in the eternal arms of faith and be wise enough to say, "I will not be disconcerted by these problems of life; I will not permit them to plunge me into doubt, and to cloud my life with vagueness and uncertainty. Man arrogates much to himself when he demands from the Infinite the full solution of all His mysteries. I will found my life on the impregnable rock of a simple fundamental truth: 'This glorious creation with its millions of wondrous phenomena pulsing ever in harmony with eternal law must have a Creator; that Creator must be omniscient and omnipotent. But that Creator Himself cannot, in justice, demand of any creature more than the best that individual can give.' I will do each day, in every moment, the best I can by the light I have; I will ever seek more light, more perfect illumination of truth, and live as best I can in harmony with the truth as I see it. If failure comes I will meet it bravely; if my pathway then lies in the shadow of trial, sorrow and suffering, I shall have the restful peace and calm strength of one who has done his best, who can look back upon the past with no pang of regret, and who has heroic courage in facing the results, whatever they be, knowing that he could not make them different."

—WILLIAM GEORGE JORDAN

Two at the Door

The end of the year is only hours away.
Soon a door will open.
This one has never been opened before.
Even now I seem to hear the noise of a key
As it is being put in the keyhole.
I know the One who will open the door.
He is the Lord of the years.
I cannot help but wonder what lies beyond
The door that is being opened.

Am I afraid? Afraid is not the word.
Interested, concerned, excited, eager,
Anxious, pensive, anticipating,
Uncertain, hopeful, fearful?
What would the word sound like
That expressed the meaning of all these?

By the knowledge of these things I am helped:
The One who is opening the door
Is He who has walked with me to it.
The One who has the key
Has told me to call Him "Father."
The One who opens saying, "Walk in,"
Will not turn and walk away.
The One who stands with me on the threshold
Does not have a worried look.
The One who has the master key
Always knows what He is doing.
The one who turned the door knob to open the door
Has been both Architect and Builder.
This One knows my name.

And now, look. The door is opening,
A bit wider with each stroke of twelve o'clock.

DECEMBER 31, 1966

Life

An Octogenarian's New Year

Many years have passed
For Octogenarians.
Each year was added
Without much thought,
Taken for granted.
Now they are valued
One by one.

This is a new year.
It is a special gift.
In some ways like the others,
But now recognized as special.
What does it hold for us?
No one knows but God,
And we do not need to know.

When I was a child,
I stretched out on the grass
And looked up at the blue sky,
And wondered: Would I live until 2000?
Now I have gone beyond it.
They have been good and fulfilling years,
And now every year is a Life's extra.

JANUARY 3, 2003

Let Us Be Real

Let us be real.
Life is good and to it we cling.
Day by day we are immersed
In the wonderful activities of living.
We revel in the joys life brings,
And we face the difficulties that come.
We work, we play, we plan,
We laugh and sometimes cry a bit.
It is only occasionally that
We lift our eyes
In the midst of swirling life
And glance into the far distance
To sense there is an inevitable end.

Then as years are added to years
We look backward and remember
Many joys and satisfactions
Interlaced with a few regrets.
The stirrings within cause us
To lift our eyes to the far horizon
And not just to give a quick glance,
But to look with clear eyes
And know with feeling there is an end.
The gift of God is offered to us
With God's outstretched hand.
And for a moment we see dimly
Through the dark curtain and glimpse
Life and activity on the other side.
It is then with a quieter peace
We complete the days God gives us.

AUGUST 13 2005

Unhappiness and Happiness

Unhappiness is the hunger to get; happiness is the hunger to give. True happiness must have the tinge of sorrow outlived, the sense of pain softened by the mellowing years, the chastening of loss that in the wondrous mystery of time transmutes our suffering into love and sympathy with others.

If the individual should set out for a single day to give happiness, to make life happier, brighter and sweeter, not for himself but for others, he would find a wondrous revelation of what happiness really is. The greatest of the world's heroes could not by any series of acts of heroism do as much real good as any individual living his whole life in seeking, from day to day, to make others happy.

—WILLIAM GEORGE JORDAN

Our Building Stones

God gives us stones to build our lives.
We can do with them what we will.

Some seek to build a structure that reaches to the sky,
And like the tower of Babel, Confusion reigns.
Some build a high containing wall
Around their selfish happiness,
To shut out the intrusion of God or man.
Some build a personal mansion of pride
And install a drawbridge over a moat,
Hoping to be safe from all alarms.
Some build a solid and ample house,
And from it are laid stepping stones
That lead into other less privileged lives,
And they daily pass over the set stones
On errands of love and mercy.

God gives us stones to build our lives.
We can do with them what we will.

OCTOBER 4, 2005

Man is the Only Animal
that Can Be Really Happy

Man is the only animal that can be really happy. To the rest of the creation belong only weak imitations of the understudies. Happiness represents a peaceful attunement of a life with a standard of living. It can never be made by the individual, by himself, for himself. It is one of the incidental by-products of an unselfish life. No man can make his own happiness the one object of his life and attain it, any more than he can jump on the far end of his shadow. If you would hit the bull's-eye of happiness on the target of life, aim above it. Place other things higher than your own happiness and it will surely come to you. You can buy pleasure, you can acquire content, you can become satisfied, but Nature never put real happiness on the bargain counter. It is the undetachable accompaniment of true living. It is calm and peaceful; it never lives in an atmosphere of worry or of hopeless struggle.

The basis of happiness is the love of something outside self. Search every instance of happiness in the world and you will find, when all the incidental features are eliminated, that there is always the constant, unchangeable element of love—love of parent for child; love of man and woman for each other; love of humanity in some form, or a great lifework into which the individual throws all his energies.

—WILLIAM GEORGE JORDAN

Things That Hunt for Our Souls

"Rescue us from all things that hunt our souls,"
Was the ancient prayer of the Eastern Church.

What are the things that hunt for our souls?
Greed, when we are too greedy
For things of this world.
Selfishness, when we put
Me, myself, and I above all else.
Envy, when we let it creep
Into our souls when we see others prospering.
Jealousy, when that sneaky feeling
Turns us green.
Pride, when our opinion of ourselves
Enables us to look down on others.
Anger, when we boil within
And are ready to lash out.
Hate, when feelings within
Solidify into a solid attitude.
Fear, when our insecurity
Erodes our faith and trust.

When the arrows from these things find us,
Our souls are wounded.
Only God can enable us to escape
The death of our souls
And bring healing to our wounded souls.

AUGUST 11, 2007

How to Keep from Losing Our Way

A Parable

In the simple matter of my daily walks North and South of the shack, I marked a path about one hundred yards long, which I called the hurricane deck. Every three paces a two-foot bamboo stick was driven into the crust, and along these poles I ultimately strung a life line. By running my hand over this, blind-man fashion I could feel my way back and forth in the worst weather; and many were the times I did it when the air was so thick with drift that I could not see past the cowling of my windproof, and the line was a thin cord through chaos.

— ADMIRAL RICHARD E. BYRD

Early and Late Days

When I was a boy
I stretched out on the green grass,
Put my hands behind my head,
Looked up at the blue sky
With floating white clouds going by.
What is beyond the blue?
What image do I see in the shape of the cloud?
An elephant? A horse? A face? Whatever?

I think of the adults around me.
Some being and doing this.
Others being and doing that.
Some successful and "somebody."
Others getting by and unknown.

Today is as far as I can see.
How many tomorrows will I have?
What will I do with them?
What will they do for me?
When will the period be put?
What will the script tell?

There were many tomorrows,
Weeks, months, years, decades of them.
I no longer stretch out on the green grass
And look at the blue sky
And notice the white clouds.
I no longer look at many tomorrows,
But I look with gratitude at many yesterdays
And give thanks to the One
I suspected was there
When my boyish mind wondered.

SEPTEMBER 2, 2004

The Value of Good Memories

Alyosha says this to the young boys about him as he tells them to remember Clusha's death:

"You must know that there is nothing higher and stronger and more wholesome and good for life in the future than some good memory, especially a memory of childhood, of home. People talk to you a great deal about your education, but some good, sacred memory, preserved from childhood, is perhaps the best education. If a man carries many such memories with him into life, he is safe to the end of his days, and if one has only one good memory left in one's heart, even that may sometime be the means of saving us."

— FYODOR DOSTOYEVSKY

September and Autumn Days

September days are good days.
Set between the heat of summer
And the beauty of autumn colors.
The changes of the season are welcome
Because it means variety, something different.
Who wants everything always to be the same?
Not me! I like the richness of variety.

Life has its September days.
They come at the end of life's season
To have a career, to work hard,
To labor at a calling or task day in and day out.
Before what may be a cold and hard winter
Are the September and autumn days.
This is the time for the gathering of the crops.
The harvest of the grain.
The ripening of the fruit.
The rewards of years of work and service
Begin to appear, and something inside says,
"It was worth it. The labor was not in vain."

Winter will eventually come,
And then the limbs of the trees will become bare,
The cold rain will come,
And the chilling wind will blow.
Then we will be warmed by the fire within.
And gather as a family around it's glow.
Finally life draws to its natural close.

But out of the cold bleak winter,
There will come another spring.
The flowers of new life will begin to grow,
And a new generation will appear on earth.
Once again the seasons will be repeated.

Life

Careers will be chosen, work will be done.
Until for the new generation
The September days will come arriving
Before the sure and certain wind.

Life goes on, and generations come and go.
But the Lord of heaven and earth,
Constant and unchanging, is forever there.
God's mercy is from everlasting to everlasting,
And God's steadfast love is true from generation to generation.

SEPTEMBER 29, 1995

Joy and Woe

Man was made for joy and woe;
And when this we rightly know
Thro the world we safely go
Joy and woe are woven fine,
A clothing for the soul divine:
Under every grief and pine
Runs a joy with silken twine.

—WILLIAM BLAKE

The Road We Choose

Now and again the road of life forks,
And often splinters into many more ways.
Then I have to make a choice.
The moving hand of time will not let me stay.
I Look, I think, I pray. Which way?

I see the road packed hard and smooth
By numberless footprints. And it is wide.
It looks almost level. But no.
It is going downward ever so slightly.

I see the road on which there are fewer footprints.
And this road is somewhat narrower.
It looks almost level. But no.
It's going upward ever so slightly.

I see other roads that beckon.
Some will circle back around,
And to follow them means
To come back to where I am now.

I see other roads that beckon.
They are trackless
Except for a footprint here and there.
I wonder: Do they lead to a trackless waste?

Then I hear a faint whisper:
"I will lead you in the path of righteousness."
And I look again at the many roads.
I choose, with the feeling of a leap of faith.

I set out on my journey.
Again the whisper: "I know the way that you take."
So I walk the road of life I have chosen.
The quiet whisper comes:
"I am with you always, to the end of time."

JUNE 19, 2009

Three Travelers

Three travelers, having neither map nor goal
   became lost along the way.
Said the first, But I was following a star . . . .
Said the second, But I was following the road. . . .
Said the third, But I was following you. . . .
   I thought you knew.
         —Clark Strand

There are three ways:
To look and to have a dream
And if the dream is as fixed as the North Star
That dream can pull us onward,
It can set our course,
It can establish our purpose,
It can shape our character.
It can define our life.
I dream a dream one day, and now. . .

To look out upon the road of life
And see a way that leads into the unknown,
And to set our feet on that road
And seek to be persistent and disciplined
And at every fork in the road
Choose carefully and wisely
Between the less traveled and the most traveled.
I chose my road one day, and now . . .

To look around and see the person I admire
And follow that person's example,
And emulate the character I see.
And ask "What would that person do in this situation?"
And observe how adversities are handled,
And see how others are treated,
And understand what is valued.
I found my hero one day, and now . . .

JULY 20, 2009

The Story of Three Brothers

The first was a Bishop, wanting to build great cathedrals to God,
    for God's glory and his, too.

The second was a dope-fiend, drunkard and wastrel, of whom the first was ashamed and did not want it to be known he was his brother.

The third had been taken to Australia when a baby and the brothers did not know anything about him at all, except two rumors:
    That he was immensely rich,
    That he was as pure as salt.

It was discovered that he was coming back. The brothers were anxious to see him.
    The first thought he might give him a million dollars to help him build the cathedral.
    The second thought he would be understood.
When they finally discovered him, he was the servant in the house, blacking the shoes, taking out the garbage, cleaning the rooms, serving.

(From a speech by George A. Buttrick,
August 28, 1955, Montreat, North Carolina)

Viewpoint

In his youth, Brooks Adams made this entry in his diary: "Went fishing with my father—the most glorious day of my life." And so great was the influence of this one day's personal experience with his father that for thirty years thereafter he made repeated references in his diary to the glowing memory of that day.

The rest of the story has a frightening aspect to it. Strangely enough, Brook's father, Charles Francis Adams, onetime ambassador to Great Britain, made a different comment, in his diary about the same day and incident: "Went fishing with my son. A day wasted."

Here we have the thrilled response of a boy to what seemed to him to be the personal interest and companionship of someone very important to him. At the same time we have the blindness of that same adult to the significance of what he was doing in terms of the power of the personal. Here is illustrated both our need of the personal and our ignorance of its power and importance.

— REUEL L. HOWE

Gifts for the Living

"Man is born to trouble as the sparks fly upward."
This ancient proverb expresses the reality
That to live is to experience troubles.
There are no exceptions.

The human spirit is remarkably resilient
As it weathers the ups and downs of life.
Three gifts nourish the spirit along the way:
Quiet courage, patient hope, unshakable trust.
These are gifts that God
Puts under the tree of life.
Open them carefully one by one,
For they are precious gifts.
God has put them there for you.

JUNE 15, 2009

Thoughts on Freedom

Man's illusion: That he is free, or can be totally free.

Man's deception: Man's so-called freedom to "do as he pleases"
    leads him into bondage to himself, his habits, and his
desires.

Man's freedom: Man's highest freedom comes in bondage to
God;
    "You shall know the truth and the truth shall make you
free."
    "Bend your necks to my yoke . . . and your souls will find
relief."

Man's choice: To follow "freedom" and have woven around
him the
    web of bondage; or to submit to the yoke of God in Christ
    and enter into the ever enlarging vistas of genuine freedom!

JULY 2, 1970

Buttercups and Bitter Weeds

My mind is fertile ground
For memories of the past.
Images of major matters come and go.
Then there are many images
Of small things that happened
As many as eighty years ago,
Their memory triggered by some
Present event or random thought.

Strange little things of the past!
Some like buttercups of the spring
And some like bitter weeds.
The buttercups give me a good feeling
A bit like I felt when the thing first happened.
The bitter weeds give me the same
Pang of hurt that I felt
When the original bitter taste was experienced.

I notice with gratitude that there
Is a garden full of buttercups
And only a scattering of bitter weeds.
I cherish the memory of the buttercups.
I seek to dismiss or put out of my mind
The bitter weeds.

JANUARY 30, 2012

Part 2

Christian Experience

The Inner Stirring

There is something stirring in me which indicates a metamorphosis. Precisely for this reason I did not dare to take the trip to Berlin—for that would be to produce an abortion. I shall therefore keep quiet, not work too hard, yea, hardly at all, not begin a new book, but try to come to myself, to think thoroughly the thought of my melancholy together with God on the spot. In that way my melancholy may be relieved and Christianity come closer to me. Hitherto I have defended myself against my melancholy by intellectual labor which keeps it at a distance—now, by faith that in forgiveness God has forgotten what guilt there is in it, I must myself try to forget it, but not by any diversion, not by any remoteness from it, but in God, so that when I think of God I may think that He has forgotten it, and thus learn for my part to date to forget it in forgiveness.

—WALTER LOWRIE, *A SHORT LIFE OF KIERKEGAARD*

The Light Within Us

Never act against the light within us.
What light? The unexplainable glow within.
It is there. Where did it come from?
It emerged from the mystery of creation.
Strange, but birds of the air
And beasts of the field
Do not appear to have it.
But as every human child
Grows into self-consciousness,
A light, dim at first ,
Begins to flicker and grow.

In that light is a sense of right and wrong.
It is what makes a child say,
"That's not fair!"
It affects the decisions we make.
It pushes back the darkness
So that we can see more clearly.
When we pay attention to it,
It becomes brighter.
We can almost extinguish it,
(But not quite)
By trying to ignore it,
By covering it over
With selfishness, greed, and pride.
When the light becomes dim
We become insensitive and calloused
And often lose our way,
Because the light within is our gyroscope.

So, never act against the light within us.
Each time we are guided by it,
It becomes brighter and brighter.
And at the end of the day
We can lie down in peace.

OCTOBER 18, 2005

The Treasures of Going Deeper

Eternal joy is the end of the ways of God. This is the message of all religions. The kingdom of God is peace and joy. This is the message of Christianity. But eternal joy is not to be reached by living on the surface. It is rather attained by breaking through the surface, by penetrating the deep things of ourselves, of our world, and of God. The moment in which we reach the last depth of our lives is the moment in which we can experience the joy that has eternity within it, the hope that cannot be destroyed, and the truth on which life and death are built. For in the depth is truth; and in the depth is hope; in the depth is joy.

—PAUL TILLICH

Something Down Deep Is Seldom Ever Reached*

Something down deep is seldom ever reached.
Like a well of deep water
With no ripples, and no noise,
It is kept and replenished
By the quiet unobserved seeping in from the sides.
But occasionally a bucket is lowered
And the quiet deep is reached.

What is the shape of the bucket?
And whose hand lowered it?
It has a varied shape:
The shape of tragedy and illness,
Of sorrow, of fear, of threat,
And also of love,
A vivid moment of communion with God,
A deep insight from God's word,
An unexpected joy.
Whose hand lowered it into the deep?
I do not really know,
But perhaps no matter whose hands they seem to be,
They are really the hands of God.

JANUARY 1971

(This is the first poem of mine that was published.
The Christian Herald, January 1971)

My Spirit Needs a Daily Bath

I take a bath every day.
My spirit needs a daily bath also.
Both my body and spirit
Are involved in day to day living.

Some days envy creeps in,
Or jealously seeps in,
Or resentment shows up,
Or faith flickers and dims,
Or worry hangs like a dark cloud,
Or selfishness becomes a priority,
Or self-righteousness infuses my being,
And a number of other things
Attach themselves to my spirit.

My spirit needs a daily bath!
An early quiet time
When I worship the living God,
Confess my sinful humanity,
Accept God's gracious mercy,
And quietly and sincerely pray:
"Create in me a clean heart, O God,
And renew a right spirit within me,"
Then my spirit feels clean
And I am ready for the living of a new day.

OCTOBER 13, 2007

When Christ Is Faced

You cannot have opinion about the Christ after you have faced him. You can only do the truth by following him or do the lie by denying him.

—PAUL TILLICH

The Fight Within

When the fight begins within himself,
A man's worth something. God stoops
O'er his head; Satan looks up between
His feet. Both tug. He's left, himself,
In the middle: the soul wakes and grows.

—ROBERT BROWNING

Great Acceptance

Mary said:
"Let it be according to your word,"
And Jesus, the Savior of the world was born.
No protesting, but quiet acceptance,
And Jesus, the Christ was born of the Virgin Mary.
The great acceptance when
The quiet "Yes" is said to God
Opens the door for the living Christ to come in.

Who am I?
A human being, and quite imperfect.
My heart is not always pure.
My actions are not always right.
My motives are often mixed.
My love of God is often cold.
My love of my neighbor is often lacking.
But wonder of wonders:
I am accepted by God! God says so!

Two great acceptances:
When I accept God, say "Yes" to God.
When I realize that God accepts me.
Then the Divine God and human person meet.

(Thoughts stirred by the readings of Karl Barth and Paul Tillich)

AUGUST 25, 2008

The Grace of Acceptance

We cannot transform our lives, unless we allow them to be transformed by that stroke of grace. It happens; or it does not happen. And certainly it does not happen if we try to force it upon ourselves, just as it shall not happen so long as we think, in our self-complacency, that we have no need of it. Grace strikes us when we are in great pain and restlessness. It strikes us when we walk through the dark valley of a meaningless and empty life. It strikes us when we feel that our separation is deeper than usual, because we have violated another life, a life which we loved, or from which we were estranged. It strikes us when our disgust for our own being, our indifference, our weakness, our hostility, and our lack of direction and composure have become intolerable to us. It strikes us when, year after year, the longed-for perfection of life does not appear, when the old compulsions reign within us as they have for decades, when despair destroys all joy and courage. Sometimes at that moment a wave of light breaks into our darkness, and it is as though a voice were saying: "You are accepted." You are accepted, accepted by that which is greater than you, and the name of which you do not know. Do not ask for the name now; perhaps you will find it later. Do not try to do anything now; perhaps later you will do much. Do not seek for anything; do not perform anything; do not intend anything. Simply accept the fact that you are accepted! If that happens to us, we experience grace. After such an experience we may not be better than before, and we may not believe more that before. But everything is transformed. In that moment, grace conquers sin, and reconciliation bridges the gulf of estrangement. And nothing is demanded of this experience, no religious or moral or intellectual presupposition, nothing but acceptance.

—PAUL TILLICH

The Ultimate Yes

I don't know who or what put the question, I don't know when it was put. I don't even remember answering. But at some moment I did answer "Yes" to Someone or Something, and from that hour I was certain that existence is meaningful and that, therefore my life, in self-surrender had a goal. From that moment I have known what it means "not to look back," and "to take no thought for the morrow."

—DAG HAMMARSKJOLD

The Way to Peace

If you do not flee your own self first, wherever it is you flee, you will find there obstacles and restlessness, be it where it may. People who seek peace in outward things, whether in places, ways, persons, works, or in flight, in poverty and abasement, or anything else however big it looks, still all they try to do is nothing, and there is no peace. They seek all amiss, who seek peace that way. The further they go out, the less will they find what they are after. They go like one who has missed his way; the further he goes, the more he strays. What then, should one do? He should leave himself first, and so he will have left all things.

—MEISTER ECKHART, QUOTED BY GEORGES A. BARROIS

How does one leave himself? It is when in the deep psyche of the spirit, the essence of being, the soul says "Yes" to God, and in that moment becomes free and on the way to peace.

AUGUST 13, 2006

The Soft Whisper of God

God spoke to Elijah in a still small voice,
Not in the wind, earthquake, and fire.
Even now there is the soft whisper of God.

There are many loud voices in the world,
That ring and clang in our ears:
Success. Achievement. Money. Power.
Loud voices cry out:
Get ahead! Have fun! Be happy!
And the soft whisper of God is not heard.

The Psalmist writes for us to be still
So that we may know God.
In stillness and quietness
We may silence the loud voices of the world,
And in the cultivated stillness and quietness,
In time we may hear
The gentle and soft whisper of God.
God whispers love, forgiveness, acceptance, and peace,
And in that soft whisper we are made whole,
And feel secure in God's good grace.

(Thoughts stirred by Thomas a Kempis'words:
"Blessed are the ears which receive the echoes of the soft whisper of God,
and turn not aside to the whisperings of the world.")

AUGUST 30, 2006

Indescribable Joy

The Saturday before the fifth Sunday after Easter, which came fifteen days after his birthday, Soren Kierkegaard made this remarkable entry, which with unaccustomed precision he dated May 19, 10:30 A.M. "There is such a thing as an indescribable joy which glows through us as unaccountably as the Apostle's outburst is unexpected: 'Rejoice, and again I say Rejoice!' . . . not a joy over this or that, but full jubilation, with hearts, and souls, and voices! I rejoice over my joy of, in, by, at, on, through, with my joy. . ..A heavenly refrain, which cuts short, as it were, our ordinary song; A joy which cools and refreshes like a breeze, a gust of the trade wind which blows from the grove of Mamre to the eternal mansions."

—WALTER LOWRIE

An Experience with God

After Captain Eddie Rickenbacker returned from his twenty-one days adrift in the Pacific, he was called on to address a large group of disabled veterans in a rehabilitation hospital. Only incidentally did he touch upon employment and business opportunities. The keynote was: "Men, if you have not had an experience with God in your life, my advice is to get busy and get yourself one."

—JOHN SUTHERLAND BONNELL

Second Conversion

His growing decision to retire from the world was confirmed on November 23, 1654, when he experienced what is known as his "second conversion." The written memorial of that experience, which he wore thereafter as a kind of amulet, records that from ten-thirty until twelve-thirty that night he knew "the God of Abraham, God of Isaac, God of Jacob, not of philosophers and scientists," and that he resolved "total submission to Jesus Christ and to my director."

—PASCAL

To Be Naked

To be naked!
I need to be naked.
No, not in that way.
My body is fully clothed,
But somewhere beyond my body
Is the essence of the real me,
The spirit, the soul that drives the body.

The spirit, the soul is usually clothed.
It is wrapped in clothing
So others cannot see the me
As I really am.
I put on pretense.
I project an image
That I want others to see.
I am not going to undress my soul
For all the world to see.

But before God it is healthy
To undress the soul.
God can see through our clothes
Of pretense anyway.
So for the health of my soul
I need to lay my soul bare
In the presence of the eternal God.
Then God may heal me,
Correct me, change me,
Or even give me the rebirth
Of a new spirit that
Makes me authentic to the core
And sets me free
To live in the security of God's love.

JUNE 24, 2006

Asking The *Questions*

Look at the student who knows the content of the hundred
most important books of world history, and yet whose
spiritual life remains as shallow as it ever was, or perhaps
becomes even more superficial. And then look at an
uneducated worker who performs a mechanical task day
by day, but who suddenly asks himself: "What does it mean,
that I do this work? What does it mean for my life? What
is the meaning of my life?" Because he asks these
questions, that man is on the way into depth, whereas
the other man, the student of history, dwells on the surface
among petrified bodies, brought out of the depth by some
spiritual earthquake of the past. The simple worker may
grasp truth, even though he cannot answer his questions;
the learned scholar may possess no truth, even though he
knows all the truths of the past.

—PAUL TILLICH

The Sense of God's Existence

That seed, which it is impossible to eradicate, a sense of the existence of a deity, yet remains; but so corrupted as to produce only the worst of fruits. Yet this is a further proof of what I now contend for, that an idea of God is naturally engraved on the hearts of men, since necessity extorts a confession of it, even from reprobates themselves. In the moment of tranquility, they facetiously mock the Divine Being, and with loquacious impertinence derogate from his power. But if any despair oppress them, it stimulates them to seek him, and dictates concise prayers, which prove that they are not altogether ignorant of God, but that what ought to have appeared before had been suppressed by obstinacy!

—JOHN CALVIN

The Pervading Presence of God

Sometimes the morning mist makes a beautiful scene.
It pervades the whole landscape.
It gently engulfs the trees,
Enveloping every trunk, limb, twig, and leaf.
Any house, barn, fence or object
Stands in the quiet grey mist.

This image seeps into my mind
As a symbol of the presence of God.
God is everywhere,
Pervading the whole scene
And leaving no detail untouched.
God is there like the mist,
Quiet and gentle.
My spirit senses God's presence.
This image helps me
To practice the presence of God
And to feel God's quiet and gentle love,
Which brings my spirit a quiet and gentle peace.

SEPTEMBER 4, 2006

A Holy Experience

(Lutheran Bishop Lajos Ordass in 1948 was arrested and imprisoned by the communist government of Hungary on trumped-up charges. Though released from prison in May, 1950, he was removed from his ecclesiastical office and thus silenced by the government. No more was heard from the bishop until late summer of 1956 when the courts of both state and church absolved him of all the earlier charges and restored to him the right to preach. So, after a lapse of more than eight years, early in October he was back in the pulpit. This is an excerpt from his first sermon preached in Budapest.)

I am speaking after a long silence now. I am not searching among memories of a long-past childhood; neither do I want to speak of the hours of happiness, but of the years of silence. And I do assert that there is a holy relationship between Jesus and the believer, comparable to the relationship between the bride and bridegroom.

When a loving couple meet and stay together, great words are exchanged, such as "My life and treasure, I love you . . . until death . . . in eternity." I have heard these words from the lips of my Lord, my dauntless and staunch Savior. He said it when I had nobody on earth. He said it when I was wholly unworthy and dejected. From the lips of my Lord—and there is no mistake—I heard clearly: "I love you, until death, in eternity. . . ." I have no doubt that he called upon me and that what he said was true.

On the whole, those of you who knew me in the past must know that I am not sentimental. No one should interpret my words in such a sense. It was a holy experience, priceless, dear, and eternal. He was with me when everyone else deserted me. When fear shook me, he took me into his strong arms and led me across a narrow plank to the shores of life's new beginning. In the black of darkness of night he let me see the message of dawn's arrival. So unbounded was my Savior's love towards me.

(FROM *THE PULPIT*, DECEMBER 1956)

Quiet Sundays

They are not quite like other days.
They are not meant to be.
Sometimes they are almost
Like just another day.

But now and then, one is special.
Something stirs within, deep within.
Is it the flutter of an angel's wing?
Is it the touch of God's living Spirit?
If it is true that God sets eternity
In the human heart,
Is the stirring within the lapping
Of the wave of eternity on the human shore?

Who knows? But something
Out of the ordinary may be happening.
Nurture that moment.
It may lead to the discovery
Of a pearl of great price.

SUNDAY, DECEMBER 15, 2002

The Kingdom of God in Our Hearts

Belief in the Kingdom of God makes the biggest demands of all the articles of the Christian faith. It means believing the seemingly impossible, the conquest of the spirit of the world by the Spirit of God. We look with confidence for the miracle to be wrought through the Spirit.

The miracle must happen in us before it can happen in the world. We dare not set our hope on our efforts to create the conditions of God's Kingdom in the world. We must indeed labor for its realization. But there can be no Kingdom of God in the world without the Kingdom of God in our hearts. The starting point is our determined effort to bring every thought and action under the sway of the Kingdom of God. Nothing can be achieved without inwardness. The Spirit of God will only strive against the spirit of the world when it has won its victory over the spirit in our hearts.

—ALBERT SCHWEITZER (E.N. MOSLEY'S *THE THEOLOGY OF ALBERT SCHWEITZER*)

Communion Thoughts

Bread and Wine.
They nourish the body.
They enter the physical body
And keep it going.
Without it the body weakens.
Without it the body ultimately dies.

Bread and Wine.
Symbols of Jesus Christ.
They nourish the spiritual body
And keep it going.
Without it the spiritual body weakens.
Without it the spiritual body ultimately dies.

What does Christ entering the spiritual body mean?
It means our spirit becomes like His spirit.
He had total faith in God the father.
To him there were no outcasts.
He reached out to the halt, blind, and maimed.
He saw the child in everyone.
He broke with tradition when it crippled human beings.
He saw hypocrisy for what it was.
He rode a donkey rather than a white stallion.
He drank his cup of suffering.
His forgiveness was limitless.
His vision penetrated the veil of death.

What does our spiritual body look like as it grows?
It grows to look like the spirit of Jesus.
Take the Christ which the bread and wine symbolize
And let him feed and nourish the spiritual body.
The more mature it becomes,
The more it resembles the spirit of Christ.

SEPTEMBER 5, 2004

The Parable of the Well

In the vast sandy Syrian desert
There is a deep, deep well.
It is marked by a circular stone base
About four feet high.
There are gashes in the stone wall
About twelve or eighteen inches deep,
Worn there in the solid rock
By ropes that have pulled up skins
Or jugs or buckets of water
By unknown and unnumbered thousands
Of thirsty people for hundreds of years.

Is the no named well
A well of Abraham or Isaac?
Is it like Jacob's well
Where Jesus refreshed himself
And told the Samaritan woman
About the living water?

In my mind I see the ancient well,
And slide my fragile rope of faith
Across the gashed stone wall
To lower my leaky vessel
Into the deep of the ancient well.
I pull up life-giving water,
As unknown thousands have done
And like the unknown thousands
Of thirsty travelers will do,
In the centuries that will come and go.

MARCH 29, 2005

Thirsty People

Thirsty people!
We are all thirsty people,
Some more than others.
The pangs of our thirst are
More poignant sometimes than at others.

Water from Jacob's well is cold and clear.
To drink from its far away depth
Both thrills and refreshes.
It excites sacred emotion,
For the place has been hallowed by our Lord.

But water from Jacob's well
Does not satisfy deeply enough,
Nor does it refresh long enough.
But there is One beside
The well from which we drink
Who offers the water for which we thirst.

"Whoever drinks of the water
That I shall give him
Will never thirst.
It will become in him
A spring of water
Welling up to eternal life."

"Sir, Master, Messiah, Lord,
Living Christ, Present God,
Give us this water!"

OCTOBER 6, 1967

The Momentary Revelation

This was a grand period; I was conscious only of a mind utterly at peace, a mind adrift upon the smooth, romantic tides of imagination, like a ship responding to the strength and purpose in the enveloping medium. A man's moments of serenity are few, but a few will sustain him a lifetime. I found my measure of inward peace then; the stately echoes lasted a long time. For the world then was like poetry—that poetry which is "emotion remembered in tranquility."

Perhaps this period was just the repeated pattern of my youth. I sometimes think so. When I was growing up, I used to steal out of the house at night, and go walking in Glass's woods, which were a little way up the road from our place. In the heavy shadows of the Shenandoah Valley hills, the darkness was a little terrifying, as it always is to small boys; but, when I would pause and look up into the sky, a feeling that was midway between peace and exhilaration would seize me. I never quite succeeded, as a boy, in analyzing that feeling, any more than I did when it used to come to me as a naval officer, in the night watches at sea, and later when, as an explorer, I first looked upon mountains and lands which no one before me had ever seen. No doubt it was partly animal: the sheer expanding discovery of being alive, of growing, of no longer being afraid. But there was more to it than just that. There was the sense of identification with vast movements; the premonition of destiny that is implicit in every man; and the sense of waiting for the momentary revelation.

—ADMIRAL RICHARD E. BYRD

Meditation

Some say they can worship in nature and do not need the Church or the ancient words of a book. I saw a man worship using nature rightly. It was in Montreat in August, 1955. I was in my room planning my sermon schedule for the coming season.

A retired minister came out on the second floor porch over-looking Susan Lake and the Assembly Inn surrounded by the beautiful rim of the Smokey Mountains. He had his Bible in his hands, but he sat for some time looking at the beauties of nature in the late Sunday afternoon. Then after a while, he opened his Bible, read some, and every once in a while he would stop and look out at the beauty of nature. He was quite alone and did not know that I or anyone was watching him. Possibly he was thinking of God, nature, God's world, God's word, and himself in relation to it all.

I was moved as I observed such worshipful meditation with nature and the Book.

Ready for the New

The new in history always comes when people least believe in it. But, certainly, it comes only in the moment when the old becomes visible as the old and tragic and dying, and when no way out is seen. We live in such a moment; such a moment is our situation. We realize this situation in its depth only if we do not continue to say, "We know where the new will come from. It will come from this institution or this movement, or this special class, or this nation, or this philosophy, or this church." None of these, of course, is excluded from being the place where the new will appear. But none of these can guarantee its appearance. All of us who have looked at one of these things as the chosen place of the new have been disappointed. The supposedly new always proves to be the continuation of the old, deepening its destructive conflicts. And so I repeat: the first thing about the new is that we cannot force it and cannot calculate it. All we can do is to be ready for it.

—PAUL TILLICH

The New Being

We, the ministers and teachers of Christianity, do not call you to Christianity, but rather to the new being to which Christianity should be a witness and nothing else, not confusing itself with that new being. Forget all Christian doctrines; forget your own certainties and your own doubts, when you hear the call of Jesus. Forget all Christian morals, your achievements and your failures, when you come to him. Nothing is demanded of you – no idea of God, and no goodness in yourselves, not your being religious, not your being Christian, not your being wise, and not your being moral. But what is demanded is only your being open and willing to accept what is given to you, the new being, the being of love and justice and truth, as it is manifest in him whose yoke is easy and whose burden is light.

—PAUL TILLICH

A New Luster to Life

It is sort of withered and dull.
It didn't happen all at once.
It just sort of got that way.
    And it didn't use to be!
    It had a glow and sparkle
    That was a fullness and brightness.
What has happened?
Nothing, really.
It just has lost its luster.

Could it be that the luster and sparkle
Was nothing more than youth
And the thrill of beginning years?
Out of the shriveled present,
Can there be another kind of luster
That will not tarnish with the years?
    A dim faith dares answer "Yes."

If when I walk the way from here to there,
    Inclined to say, "But we had hoped . . .,"
If when I do not understand
And am slow of heart to believe,
If in the simple daily events of life,
    Like in the breaking of bread,
If in the dark lonely hours before the dawn
    When love seems to have grown cold . . .

Then, especially then, if He will answer
With the warmness of his presence,
And my yearning spirit can touch
    Just the hem of his garment in faith,
And if the ears of my spirit can hear:
 "Lo I am with you always,
Even to the end of the world,"

Then I shall become alive!
Not with the aliveness of the years,
But with the aliveness of eternity.

(Luke 24:13–35)

APRIL 13, 1967

The Lisping God

For who, even of the meanest capacity, understands not, that God lisps, as it were, with us, just as nurses are accustomed to speak to infants?

—JOHN CALVIN

Thought Talk

Belief: God is real.
        I am real.

Question: Any contact?

Contact Places: Spirit upon spirit
        Written word
        Living word
        Fellow man
        Experiences
        Worship

Question: Contact making any difference?

Unbelievable: That contact with God
        would make no difference.

Gift: Time. Quantity unknown.

My Chance: To be open. To worship.
        To think. To meditate.
        To yearn for contact, for relationship.
My freedom: To make no contact.

Unavoidable: The consequences.

MARCH 2, 1971

The Yearning to be Cured

Human beings need God.
Every human being needs God!
"Our souls are restless,
Until they find rest in Thee."
We are made that way!

My restlessness? What helps?
Friends! Activity! Church! Amusements!
Yes, they help for a while.
But what am I after?
Distraction from my restlessness?
    All distraction is so temporary!
Escape from my restlessness?
    There is no final escape from my deepest self,
    And I always come back to my restlessness.
Cure for my restlessness?
    Ah! This is my hunger!
    And God, only God satisfies.

I am like a house.
There are so many doors and windows,
And even cracks in my walls.
God can come inside through any opening.

FEBRUARY 23, 1971

The Healing Power of Love

In the Battle Creek Sanitarium this experiment was carried out. A dog with a happy disposition worked his way into everyone's affections at the Sanitarium. He was irresistible. The doctors operated on him and found that the marrow in his bones was a beautiful pink—it was filled with red corpuscles. The wound healed almost immediately. Then word was passed down the line that the dog was to be treated with indifference. No one was to pay any attention to him. Some repulsed his advances with gruffness. The dog pined away under this changed treatment. He would stay under tables and sofas. His spirits dropped. Again he was operated on. The marrow in his bones was found to be a dull brown, almost bereft of red corpuscles. The wound healed very slowly, and infection was feared. Then the treatment changed. Everybody was instructed to be friendly again. The dog responded very slowly to this renewed friendship. He had been let down once, so he was suspicious. But he finally responded, and his spirits returned. His tail began wagging; he was his joyous self again. Once more he was operated on, and this time his marrow was again a healthy pink and full of red corpuscles. Again the wound healed quickly. It was obvious that the emotional states of the dog changed the very marrow in his bones. This illustrates what can happen to the health of a human being when subjected to wrong treatment by society, or thrown off balance by his own wrong reactions to life.

—E. STANLEY JONES

The Archimedean Point

From him (Soren Kierkegaard's father) I learned what Father-love is, and I got a conception of the divine father-love, the one unshakable thing in life, the true Archimedean point.

—WALTER LOWRIE, *A SHORT LIFE OF KIEKEGAARD*

Who Would Ever Run Off the Gentle Jesus?

The words they said to Jesus are shocking:
Go away! Leave us alone! Get out of our country!
Did somebody say these words to Jesus?
Yes, when a wild man was tamed and swine were drowned.
To Jesus who was so gentle and kind?
Why, he never hurt anyone!
He touched the little children,
He healed the sick, restored sight to the blind,
Gave power to walk to the crippled,
Brought hope to the poor and prisoner,
Quieted the crying and sorrowful,
And showed a new way for mankind.

Ah! It was the new way that did it!
He put people before things.
    No telling what would happen in a community
    If profit and property were made secondary to people.
He put spirit before form.
    Too many old familiar forms and structures
    Might be altered or discarded if that were done.
He put love before orthodoxy.
    Our inherited answers have become our neat traditions,
    And what will putting love of God and man first do to them?
He put people before rules.
    This "Sabbath is made for man" talk
    Releases an idea that will ruin our rules.
He put serving before being served.
    From the beginning the weak have served the strong,
    And now he talks of first honor to those who serve.

Sure, He is gentle and kind,
And we don't mind him helping here and there.
But the trouble is that he turns everything upside down!
You don't really blame some of us
For wanting to keep him out, do you?

JANUARY 25, 1971

Deep Calm

The sea ebbs and flows with waves large and small.
The fury of wind and storm
Agitate only the surface of the sea.
They may penetrate two or three hundred feet,
But below that is the calm unruffled deep.

Life goes on from day to day
Like restless waves out at sea
And their gentle lapping on the shore.
But there are days when the strong winds blow
And occasionally with the fury of a storm.
Then we are troubled, agitated, and anxious.
We are ruffled and disturbed and maybe scared.

The human spirit has the capacity for great depth.
When at our deepest level there is a strong faith
In the eternal God of love,
It brings a deep down calmness
That gives us stability
When the strong and stormy winds
That come to all on life's journey
Disturbs and test our spirits.

(Thoughts stirred by William George Jordan, *The Majesty of Calmness*)

JULY 11, 2008

Toward the End

Toward the end of life things change,
Not suddenly or radically
But quietly and slowly.
The strong challenges have slackened.
Life seems to settle a bit
And sort itself out,
Where priorities get recognized.
We can "let go" of some things,
And in quietness we can
Absorb a gentle peace
As the restlessness of "doing" subsides.

We have basically done what we could.
There have been mistakes, failures,
Misjudgments, and the fallout from conflicts.
We could have done better here and there.
But we can learn to do
What the apostle Paul advises: Forget the past.
And in its place a growing sense of gratitude
Seeps into our souls.

OCTOBER 11, 2006

Family

At the end only two things really matter to a man, regardless of who he is; and they are the affection and understanding of his family. Anything and everything else he creates are insubstantial; they are ships given over to the mercy of the winds and tides of prejudice, but the family is an everlasting anchorage, a quiet harbor where a man's ships can be left to swing to the moorings of pride and loyalty.

—ADMIRAL BYRD

Interaction with Christ

Christ can be approached in the same way if He is the one whom Christians say He is, the true image of the loving God. If we can communicate with other elements of the spiritual world through dream images, then we can also interact with the image of Christ and the reality which He incorporates and expresses. Of all the processes of imagination which have helped me, none has offered half as much value as this approach to Christ. Several times a week I simply stop and wait before Him, sometimes picturing Him at the time of the resurrection, rising victorious from the tomb, or perhaps knocking at the door of my soul , as William Hunt's picture, "The Light of the World," suggests. And then in the quiet I say, "Here I am. Tell me what you wish of me."

At first the interchange may seem forced and unreal. Often I wonder if I am making up the answers that come out of the silence. And then within me something clicks. There is a change, and suddenly I know that I am not talking to myself. There is a voice other than my own, the voice of someone who cares about me, one who speaks to my deepest problems and fears, one who heals my wounds and restores my courage. Often I ask Him why He bothers to come and be with someone like me. Each time He tells me that He is Love and that it is the nature of Love to give of itself, that He cares for every human being and comes whenever we will allow Him to enter and share Himself with us. This experience is one that is never exhausted. It returns each time as fresh and real and autonomous as a magnificent sunset or an encounter with a truly loving human being. One can never predict what the meeting will bring.

—MORTON KELSEY

Gifts for Living

"Man is born to trouble as the sparks fly upward."
This ancient proverb expresses the reality
That to live is to experience troubles.
There are no exceptions.

The human spirit is remarkably resilient
As it weathers the ups and downs of life.
Three gifts nourish the spirit along the way:
Quiet courage, patient hope, unshakable trust.
These are the gifts that God
Puts under the tree of life.
Open them carefully one by one,
For they are precious gifts.
God had put them there for you.

JUNE 15, 2009

Touch Me, Lord

In the quiet and still morning hours,
Touch me, Lord.
Touch my heart and let it beat with love.
Touch my spirit and make it lively.
Touch my will and make it obedient.
Touch my mind and make it clear.

Purify my motives.
Ignite my faith.
Enliven my hope.
Warm my love.
Strengthen my courage.
Forgive my sins.

Touch my whole being
That I may be whole,
So that I may fulfill
The chief end of life:
To glorify God and enjoy him forever.

Then when the evening hours come
And the day is done,
Touch me with gratitude
And let me lie down with your
Touch of gentle peace.

FEBRUARY 20, 2010

Part 3

Religion

The Eternal Essential Truth

Christianity Has declared itself to be the eternal essential truth which has come into being in time. It has proclaimed itself as the *Paradox,* and it has required of the individual the inwardness of faith in relation to that which stamps itself as an offense to the Jews and a folly to the Greeks—and an absurdity to the understanding. It is impossible more strongly to express the fact that subjectivity is truth, and that the objectivity is repellent, repellent even by virtue of its absurdity. And indeed it would seem very strange that Christianity should have come into the world merely to receive an explanation; as if it had been somewhat bewildered about itself, and hence entered the world to consult that wise man, the speculative philosopher, who can come to its assistance by furnishing the explanation.

— SOREN KIERKEGAARD

Idols Made with Minds, Not Hands

The absurdity of making an object
Of wood, stone, or metal
And putting it in a place of reverence
And praying to it!
Who would expect it would have power
To do anything?
The ancients did, but not
We enlightened moderns.

We worship the living God
Who is far beyond
Our infinite minds to conceive.
Out of Job's unexplainable suffering
He sensed that he knew
But the outskirts of God's ways.
And that he had heard
Only a small whisper of Him.

Jesus shows us more of God
Than man had ever seen before.
But when we become arrogant
To think we can wrap
Our minds around God
And define and contain Him,
And that He is just as we say He is,
We have made an idol with our minds.

FEBRUARY 8, 2003

Not Intellectual Doubt, But Rebellion

Until this moment Soren Kierkegaard was able to flatter himself with the notion that his defection from Christianity and from the ethical life was due to intellectual doubt and was therefore something rather superior, something Faustic. Now he learned to know that it was rebellion. Hereafter this was his constant interpretation and we may be sure that it reflected his own experience. In 1847 he wrote in the Journal: "They would have us believe that objections against Christianity come from doubt. This is always a misunderstanding. Objections against Christianity come from insubordination, unwillingness to obey, rebellion against all authority. Therefore, they have hitherto been beating the air against the objectors, because they have fought intellectually with doubt, instead of fighting ethically with rebellion . . . . So it is not properly doubt but insubordination. In vain do they try to bring the machinery into action, for the ground is bog or quicksand."

—WALTER LOWRIE, *A SHORT LIFE OF KIERKEGAARD*

To Whom Shall We Go?

Terrorists. War. Uncertainty.
Poverty. Hunger. Suffering.
Disease. Misery. Death.
Where are answers?
Where is help?
To whom shall we go?

There are options.
To the living God of the universe,
Though a God not fully known
By the smartest, wisest, and most religious
Of earthly human beings.
But in Jesus we have a clue.

There are options.
To a God we have formed
In our minds from fragments
Of Sunday School teaching in childhood,
From elements of America's civil religion,
A small God who leaves us empty.

There are options.
To no God at all.
Let misery be unanswered.
Let evil take over the globe.
Let us be animals to hurt and devour,
With no reaching for faith and hope.

I choose the first option.
I clutch at the outskirts of God's ways.
I listen for the whisper of God's voice.
I focus my image of God through Jesus.
My reason runs its course and fails.
Faith is the word God whispers to me.

FEBRUARY 13, 2003

The Invitation

The invitation halts at the parting of the ways where the paths of sin veers, for the last time, and is lost to view...in perdition. Oh, turn about, turn about, come hither! Shriek not at the difficulty of the journey back, however hard it be; fear not the toilsome path of conversion, however laboriously it leads to salvation, where as sin with winged speed, with ever increasing velocity, leads onward . . . or downward, so easily, with such indescribable ease, as easily indeed as when a horse, relieved entirely of the strains of pulling, cannot with all his might bring the wagon to a halt which thrust him over into the abyss. Be not in despair at every relapse, which the God of patience possesses patience enough to forgive and which a sinner might well have patience enough to be humbled under. Nay, fear nothing and despair not. He who says, "Come hither," is with you on your way; from Him come help and forgiveness in the path of conversion which leads to Him; and with Him there is rest.

—SOREN KIERKEGAARD

When the Soul Clicks with God

When rocks shift deep within the earth,
It has an effect on the earth's surface.
We call it an earthquake.

When a person's soul shifts and clicks with God,
Major things happen to the whole person.
Some call it conversion.
That makes a difference
In how the person views the world,
And how the person lives in the world.
Sometimes the change is radical,
And often a paradox emerges.
Torn loose from the world's attachments,
There arises a new and painful
Concern for the world, after the pattern of:
God so loved the world.

As the soul clicks with God,
God losses the chains of attachment to the world
And hurls the world into our hearts
Where with God we love it
With concern, faith, and hope.

(Thoughts stirred by reading from *A Testament of Devotion*
by Thomas   R. Kelly)

NOVEMBER 4, 2006

The Significance of a Religious Outlook

The most productive form of universal symbol systems is religion. This is why Jung was so deeply interested in religion and so sure that the greatest need of mankind is to find an adequate religious faith and understanding. There is a familiar quotation in *Modern Man in Search of a Soul,* which highlights this:

Among all my patients in the second half of life—that is to say, over thirty-five— there has not been one whose problem in the last resort was not that of finding a religious outlook on life. It is safe to say that every one of them feel ill because they had lost that which the living religions of every age have given to their followers, and none of them has been really healed who did not regain his religious outlook. This of course has nothing to do with a particular creed or membership of a church.

—A. C. OUTLER

The Way Between Two Ways

There are two ways against which I struggle.
One is narrow, rigid, and literalistic.
It is the way of easy ready-made pat answers.
It knows the size and shape of every problem,
And every solution has its one-two-three.

The other is a vague general air of religion.
It is the way which has never been seen,
For everything looks the same.
There are no markers, and anything goes.
"Walk where you will in the over soul of love,
For aren't we all trying to get to the same place?"

The trouble with way one is:
It seems so simple and sure,
But it is like being in soft concrete
Which quickly hardens.
It is a trap in which
There is little aliveness and meager freedom.

The trouble with way two is:
It is so deceptive, promising easy freedom,
But it is like an ever softening quicksand
In which one sinks
Into meaningless sameness
With a simple expression of "unknowingness."

In between these two is a way.
It has sufficient firmness for faith,
And markers to be read.
It gives enough freedom for healthy growth,
Enough direction for meaningful action,
And it leads somewhere.

MAY 27, 1971

Losing Beliefs

Professor Summer put it this way:
"I never consciously gave up a
religious belief. It was as if I had
put my beliefs into a drawer, and
when I came again to look for
them the drawer was empty."

—E. STANLEY JONES

The Sacred and the Secular

I live in two worlds: the sacred and the secular.
I hold both the sacred and the secular,
One in each extended hand, separate and apart.
When I enter the temple of religion
I leave outside the secular.
When I emerge from the temple of religion
I pick up the secular again,
Leaving the religion inside.
No wonder I can pray in the temple
And curse in the streets.

Something is not quite right.
Can I not get the religious and secular mixed,
So that there is one tapestry of life
Where both are intertwined?
Then the spirit of religion is woven
Into the fabric of the secular,
And the earthiness of the secular
Woven into the fabric of religion.
Then the secular would reflect
The pattern of the spirit,
And the religious would reflect
The reality of life in the world.

(Thoughts stirred by the way the ancient Celtic Scots in the
Hebrides Islands combined the sacred and secular in life)

OCTOBER 21, 2006

Jesus

Here is a man who was born in an obscure village. He never wrote a book. He never held an office. He never went to college. He never traveled two hundred miles from the place where he was born. He never did one of those things that usually accompany greatness. Nineteen centuries have come and gone. Today, he is the centerpiece of the human race and the leader of the column of progress. I am far within the mark when I say that all the armies that ever marched, all the navies that were ever built, all the parliaments that ever sat, and all the kings that ever reigned, put together have not affected the life of man upon this earth as powerfully, as has that one solitary life.

ATTRIBUTED TO PHILLIPS BROOKS

God Is Both Father and Mother

A father loves in big patterns.
His child needs a house to live in,
Some games to play,
Some work to do,
An education for the tasks of life.
This requires protection and care,
And the money to provide.

A mother loves in smaller patterns.
Her child needs arms around him and her,
Tears understandingly wiped away,
Youthful enthusiasm shared,
The right food for every day,
Character traits gently molded,
And good habits developed bit by bit.
This requires the daily touch of loving care.

God loves in all these patterns.
His children live in a complex world,
Where huge movements and issues
Threaten to crush and cripple.
God's children need the security of a loving providence,
And the daily touch of gentle love.
They need their failures understood,
And their dreams to be believed in.

God's children need love's patterns,
Both large and small.
God is both father and mother,
Surrounding us with the framework of providence,
And enfolding us in the love of daily care.

MAY 6, 1971

Part 4

Faith

Bread for Life

The man is empty inside.
His body is fat and his stomach is full,
But he is empty inside.
How shall I help him?
What shall I say to him?
"Eat, drink and be merry for tomorrow
You shall forget your emptiness!"
Dare I say this cruel word
While he is perishing for the lack of
The Living Bread, whom to eat is to hunger no more?

The child is crying.
So are his mother and father,
But their tears are running down inside.
The child cries because he is empty.
The parents cry not because of their hunger
But because of their child's hunger.
How shall I help them?
"Take this loaf or take this dollar."
Their voices say thanks,
But their faces ask of tomorrow.
What shall I say to this question?
Dare I tell them that my Christ loves them
And leave them to eat promises?

FEBRUARY 9, 1971

The Dark

Which of you fears the Lord and obeys his—commands?
　The man who walks in the dark with no light,
　　Yet trusts in the name of the Lord,
　　　and leans on his God.

(ISAIAH 50:10)

Every person walks in the dark.
We may see what is happening today,
But even then there is a fog
Because we do not know what
May happen before the day is over.
We may see into tomorrow and more tomorrows,
But the farther we look into the future,
The thicker the fog gets, and ultimately
We can see nothing—all dark.

Then we who walk in the dark
Where there is no light,
And who believe in the Lord
And lean on God,
Will first experience faith,
And as faith matures
It becomes trust.

And trust will take us through the dark
Until the darkness disappears
And the light of eternal life
Lets us see clearly,
And there will be no more darkness.

JULY 12, 2008

Darkness and the Candle

The darkness comes at evening time.
It comes silently and gradually.
It comes from nowhere,
And yet it seems to come from everywhere.
In the summers it alerts the katydids,
And the lightening bugs turn on their lights.
In the winter it comes cold and hard
With an almost deathly steely silence.
It enters into every nook and cranny,
And deep into the blossom of every flower.
It casts no shadow but engulfs everything,
And in the darkness everything looks the same.
It seems to be a powerful invasive phenomenon
That comes with inevitability.

But as pervasive and all encompassing as it is,
It cannot put out the light of a single candle,
For "the light shines in the darkness,
And the darkness has not put it out." *
   And it never will!

*John 1:5

JULY 28, 2008

Fear

Fear is, above all, fear of the unknown; and the darkness of the unknown is filled with the images created by fear. This is true even with respect to events on the plane of daily life: the unknown face terrifies the infant; the unknown will of the parent and the teacher creates fear in the child; and all the unknown implications of any situation or new task produce fear, which is the feeling of not being able to handle the situation. All this is true to an absolute degree with respect to death—the absolutely unknown; the darkness in which there is no light at all, and in which even imagination vanishes; that darkness in which all acting and controlling cease, and in which everything which we were is finished; the most necessary and impossible idea at the same time; the real and ultimate object of fear from which all other fears derive their power, that fear overwhelmed even Christ at Gethsemane.

—PAUL TILLICH

Fear and Faith

There are three phrases carved in the mantle of an old English home, over the fireplace:

Fear knocked at the door!

Faith answered!

There was nobody there!

—GEORGE A. BUTTRICK

A Little String of Faith

I wrapped a difficult package with a string.
The string was small and easily broken.
I thought that maybe it would not hold.
So I put another length of string
Around the package,
Then another and another
Until the package was securely wrapped.

I wrapped a small string of faith
Around a difficult situation.
It did not seem to be strong enough to hold.
So I put another fragile string of faith
Around the situation,
And kept wrapping it around and around
Until the situation was securely wrapped.

OCTOBER 19, 2006

Faith Rekindled

In earlier times faith burned with some passion,
But now faith seems to be smoldering
With hardly a glow beneath the ashes
That have accumulated over the years.
Hopes and dreams, aspirations and challenges
Kept the flames of faith burning
And sometimes bursting forth into flames.
But underneath the grey ashes
There are still the warm red embers of faith
That when stirred may have more heat
Than the flashing and leaping flames
Of a new and early faith.

The One who gave the gift of faith in earlier years
Can kindle the fires of faith again.
The Christ who called to the dead Lazarus
And brought him forth from the tomb
Can call forth the dying embers of faith,
And in their stirring we can feel again
The radiant warmth of a living faith.

SEPTEMBER 20, 2006

Hearsay or Experience

Thomas Chalmers was quite content for years to preach a cold, dry, formal religion, until one day in the manse at Kilmany, the south winds of God blew upon his heart, and from that hour he preached to save. He said, "Mathematician as I was, I had forgotten two magnitudes—the shortness of time and the vastness of eternity." But Christ had gripped him, and the dead gospel came alive. It had hands and feet now, and a heart throbbing like the heart of Jesus.

FROM A SERMON BY JAMES S. STEWART

Soliloquy of the Soul

Where art Thou, Lord?
If I knew where you were
   I would make the journey!

This world needs you.
   It seems always in strife,
   Hates run deep,
   Hurts are real.
Your Church needs you.
   Some within it are talking
      As if you were dead!
My family and I need you.
   Living can be very difficult,
   Aloneness can be very lonesome.

You have been here!
There are numerous signs
   That you have been here!

I thought I heard somebody.
It was just a friend who walked by.
He carries an impossible load—
But the way he lives in his world
   And his Church—
It seems like someone else is carrying
   The heaviest part of the load!

I am sure he didn't say anything,
   But for a moment I thought
      I heard him say one word—faith.

Thank you, God, for being here—right here.
I need you. We need you.

AUGUST 11, 1966

Four Things

Four things I pray for:
Faith, Trust, Wisdom, and Strength.

Faith is a gift.
Trust is a stance.
Wisdom is an insight.
Strength is within.

Faith is to believe in the light
   When it is dark.
Trust is to depend on God
   When there is nothing visible
   Or tangible to depend on.
Wisdom is seeing between right and wrong,
   Between the true and the false,
   Between the permanent and the temporary,
   Between the profound and the superficial.
Strength is staying in there.
   It is carrying the load,
   It is taking the next step and the next,
   It is holding on by the finger tips,
   It is the muscle of the spirit.

Four things I pray for daily:
Faith, Trust, Wisdom and Strength.

SEPTEMBER 5, 2004

The Edge of Trust

It begins with belief in God.
Not *a* God, but the eternal
God of all there is.
Then when belief accepts
That God is good,
Something in the human spirit grows.

Out of such belief faith grows.
Faith is that which enables us
To see that which is not now
And tells us that it can be.
Faith may be weak and fragile,
But it can become strong and tough.

As faith becomes more mature
We may reach up and feel
The edge of trust which is
Undergirded by belief and faith.
Then we may climb up from
The edge of trust
To the level of solid trust.

Then there emerges
A sense of security and stability,
And each day may be faced
With a deep, quiet confidence
    And serenity.

SEPTEMBER 19, 2008

The Faith Star

Darkness.
Bits of light. Perhaps stars.
A star.
A morning star. An evening star.
The star.
The star of the wise men's unlikely journey.
The star of Bethlehem's dark streets.
The star over the manger and a child.
The star of Christ! Jesus Christ!

Darkness.
Bits of faith. Twinkling faith.
A faith.
A beginning faith. An ending faith.
The faith.
The faith of wise men who follow.
The faith while in the cities' dark streets.
The faith humble and pure as clean hay
   And a baby.
The faith of Christ! Jesus Christ!

DECEMBER 12, 1968

Praying in a Stable

My father's second child and oldest daughter was very, very sick. The doctor had done all he could, and it looked as if she was going to die. With his simple faith my father went down to the barn and into a stable and got into the trough and prayed for his daughter Bettie that she would get well. She did. When my father later told me about this, I asked why he went to the stable and got in the trough? He said, "Jesus was born in a stable and laid in a manger, and I wanted to get as close to him as I could."

A Light Snow Came Last Night

A light snow came last night.
It is pretty, but not like a good snow
That covers everything with a soft white.
Green grass sticks through here and there.
The roads and walks are clear.
The temperature hovers just above freezing.
The clouds spit a bit of snow every now and then,
Like they can't decide between "enough for now"
Or 'let's give a real snow for Christmas."

In a sense the situation is very much life like.
The partial snow making some things beautiful,
But leaving some spots bare and untouched.
The snow clouds hang there,
Yet to reveal whether they will cover everything
    with white beauty
Or leave everything as it is.
So as we live with touches of beauty
And areas of bare and hard reality,
We wait for what the future holds.
But we know it will hold this:
Snow, rain, sunshine, cold, warmth, darkness,
Brightness, winter, spring, summer, and fall.
And God is there in and through it all.

DECEMBER 23, 1993

Never Alone

During one of the Scottish wars, it was often not possible to have communion in the church. One day a group of the Covenanters had spread the cloth on the heather and were celebrating the Communion there in the field. Suddenly the enemy was spotted on the horizon and the meeting came to an abrupt end, but the leader called to them to wait a moment and said this final word to them, speaking of Christ going with each one of them:

Wherever one goes there will be a second,

Wherever two goes there will be a third,

Wherever three goes there will be a fourth,

   You will never go alone.

(From a speech by Professor James S. Stewart,
August 1955, Richmond, Virginia)

A Family Verse

Trust in the Lord with all thine heart,
And lean not unto thine own understanding.
In all your ways acknowledge him,
And he will direct your paths.

—PROVERBS 3:5–6

This is the Scott family's verse that was handed down to them
by their ancestor, Agnes Irvine Scott, for whom Agnes Scott College,
in Decatur, Georgia, is named.

The Lap of God

A little girl plays with her favorite toy.
The mother sits by
And watches with the love
That only a mother can have.
The little girl goes to her mother
And puts the toy in her lap.
This toy is special
And she wants her mother to keep it
While she turns to play with her other toys.

Each of our loved ones is special to us.
Let us, with a childlike trust,
Carefully put each one
In the lap of God.

DECEMBER 12, 2009

Part 5

Providence

Faith in Providence

No security is guaranteed to anyone; no house, no work, no friend, no family, no country anywhere in the world is safe, no plans are certain of fulfillment, all hopes are threatened.

—PAUL TILLICH

The content of the faith in providence is this: When death rains from heaven as it does now, when cruelty wields power over nations and individuals as it does now, when hunger and persecution drives millions from place to place as they do now, and when prisons slums all over the world distort the humanity of the bodies and souls of men as they do now—we can boast in that time, and just in that time, that even all of this cannot separate us from the love of God.

—PAUL TILLICH

We Are Not in Charge

We are not in charge.
We are not in charge of life.
We are not in charge of much about life.
O, we can do many things,
And we are responsible for many things,
But in the final analysis,
We are not really in charge.

Life is set up in such a manner
That suffering and death are in its pattern.
We have the capacity to bring on suffering
And even hold back death for a time.
But there are limits to what we can do.
Concerning all ultimates,
And many not so ultimates,
We are not really in charge.

What does one do who does not believe in God?
How does one live who does not believe in God?
If not God, then who or what is in charge?
Are we but living in a dim light
While all around there is nothing
But the dark unknown
Out of which there comes
Unexplainable blast of wind
Or the cruel blow of a whip?
If I so believe,
It is no wonder that I am a cynic.
It is no wonder that life has no meaning.
It is no wonder I am filled
With a mixture of "I don't care" and fear.

I am not in charge of much,
And about me there is much darkness.
But for me to live I must believe
Someone is there.
The One who is there is wiser than I,
And Jesus said He knows my name and loves me.
In this faith, I can live.

JULY 10, 1968

When To Leave Events in the Hand of God

On the night of July 10–11, 1943, a vast armada of 3,000 ships containing 80,000 Allied soldiers sailed across the waters from Malta to the shores of Sicily in a great amphibious operation. General Eisenhower, surrounded by his staff officers, stood on a high hill overlooking the Malta harbor. In the light of a full moon shining down on the sea he watched the troop-laden ships weigh anchor and sail out into the mists while squadrons of planes roared into the sky. Deeply moved, Eisenhower sprang to attention and saluted his heroic men. Then he bowed his head in silent prayer—his staff joining him in this brief act of devotion. Turning to an officer beside him, Eisenhower said: "There comes a time when you've used your brains, your training, your technical skill, and the die is cast and the events are in the hands of God, and there you have to leave them."

— JOHN SOUTHERLAND BONNELL

Knowing It Is Coming

On the little island of Cayman Brac
The scuba diving is wonderful.
The beauty of the coral,
The sight of fish of many colors,
The thrill of an occasional dolphin,
The wonder and adventure of it all.
It is life and its goodness.

In the distance a storm is gathering.
Its winds pick up slowly
As it moves toward Cayman Brac.
The winds twist and turn
And make their way northward,
Stirring up the already restless seas.
It is coming to Cayman Brac for sure.
There are no planes or boats
To take us away and out of its path.
We board up the windows,
We make sure we have food and water.
We find our flashlights and check their batteries.
We wonder how strong the winds will blow.
We remember that other storms have been survived.

Life has been good and happy,
With a few squalls here and there.
Time and younger years go by,
And aging years are on the way.
There are no planes or boats
To take us out of their path
As the winds blow and the waters rise.

So we give attention to the weak places.
We check the food and water
That we need to nourish the spirit.

Providence

We plug in to recharge our batteries
To make sure of light for the darkness.
We wonder how strong the winds will blow.
We remember that other storms have been survived.
The storm most surely comes,
But just as surely it also passes.
The skies are clear and blue.
The waters are teeming with beauty and life,
And we have entered a brave new world
To experience the wonder and adventure of it all.
With faith and trust we survived and arrived.

(Written on the occasion of daughter Betty scuba diving
at Cayman Brac at the time of hurricane Charlie)

AUGUST 12, 2004

What God Has Done For Me

Saint Patrick: Therefore, I, first a rustic, a fugitive, unlearned, indeed, not knowing how to provide for the future—but I know this most certainly, that before I was humbled I was like a stone lying in deep mud; and He who is mighty came, and in His own mercy raised me, and lifted me up, and placed me on the top of the wall.

(From *The Writings of Patrick, The Apostle of Ireland*)

An Event That Matters

There is an historic incident from the story of Oliver Cromwell and John Hampden, those two stalwart makers of England. It was in the days when they were still almost unknown. So utterly weary and impatient had they grown of the way in which king and court and government were ruining the nation and bringing it down to decadence and disaster that they decided there was only one course left for them to take, and that was to leave the country and never set foot in it again. Memories of the Mayflower's intrepid adventure kept urging them, and their thoughts turned longingly to the new colony beyond the seas where the winds of freedom blew and life was clean.

One day news came to them that a ship lying in the Thames was shortly to make the Atlantic crossing. Quietly and unobtrusively Cromwell and Hampden took their places on board. Everything was in readiness for the long voyage; the two men had shaken from their feet the dust of the land whose downfall that lamented, when, at the last moment, messengers dashed up with orders from the king that on no account were they to be allowed to sail. Baulked and frustrated and angry at their fate, Cromwell and Hamden came ashore; it was the ruin of their hope. But it was that ruin that gave Cromwell to England, and shaped the subsequent course of history. Had not God, even in the wreck of the man's plans, been going on in the front?

—JAMES S. STEWART

Light on the Past and Future

If we could choose, it would be better
To have more light on the future
Than on the past.
But the reality is there is more light
On the past than on the future.

The past is illuminated by hindsight.
We see the turns we have taken
And also the turns we have missed.
We can see the terrain over which we have come
The mountains and the valleys,
The rivers we have crossed,
And the deserts we have endured.
We can recall the times when darkness was deep
And when there was brightness of day.
We can see things we are pleased we did,
And things we wish we had or had not done.

But the future?
Like with the headlights of the car,
We can see some things immediately ahead,
But only so far, beyond is the unseen.
It helps to have a destination in mind.
From the journey of the past
We have learned some things
About how to travel.

So for the unseen and unknown future
We have some confidence
Because of choices and experiences of the past.
Maybe we do not need to see all of the future
As clearly as we see the past.
Maybe it is far better that we do not.
Our future journey can be illuminated

Providence

> By faith and trust
> As we travel one day at the time.

FEBRUARY 8, 2006

He Knows the Way That I Take

Behold, I go forward, but he is not there;
And backward, but I cannot perceive him;
On the left hand I seek him, but I cannot behold him;
I turn to the right hand, but I cannot see him.
But he knows the way that I take;
When he has tried me, I shall come forth as gold.

—JOB 23:8-10

God's Steadfast Love

The Bible says,
"The steadfast love of the Lord
Is from everlasting to everlasting."
"His steadfast love endures forever."

My mind stretches to take it in.
Strong, solid, invariable love
Forever, and ever and ever.
It is like the Rocky Mountains
Reaching toward the sky,
Immovable and unvarying.
I look away and turn back again,
And they are still there
Immovable and unchanged.

God's steadfast love is forever there,
A concept larger than I can comprehend.
But His steadfast, immovable, unchanging love
Is here now and will be here
Through all the day long.
That I can grasp and be grasped by.

JANUARY 23, 2006

The Pages in the Book of Life Keep Turning

The pages in the book of life keep turning.
Sometimes they seem to turn slowly,
And at other times they flip rapidly,
Turned by the moving wind of time.

Some chapters of the past stand out.
Others fade and are little remembered.
New pages bring new chapters.
They are turned by measured time
While we eagerly read them with fear and hope.

The longer we live, the thicker the book gets.
Perhaps it is a mercy that we are forbidden
From turning to read the last chapter,
Though our curiosity makes us wonder what it tells.
It is a good gift to turn and read each new page
With interest, excitement, and anticipation.

Our faith tells us God was there at the beginning
And that God will be there at the end.
Our faith also tells us that God's hand
Was in the turning of today's page
And will be in the turning of each page
Until the final sentence is written
And the final period is carefully placed.

SEPTEMBER 7, 1995

Part 6

Adversities

Adversities

In 1847 he wrote: "it is an instance of God's grace to a man when precisely in the experience of adversities he shows that he is so fortunately constituted that like a rare musical instrument the strings not only remain intact through every new adversity, but he acquires in addition a new string on his string-board." Two years later he referred to the same figure: "It was the tension of reality which put a new string in my instrument"; and again: "As an author I have acquired a new string to my instrument, I have become capable of producing tones I otherwise never would have dreamt of."

—WALTER LOWRIE, *A SHORT LIFE OF KIEKEGAARD*

Helpful Pain

Hodding Carter was an outstanding newspaper editor in Greenville, Mississippi, during the era of the Civil Rights struggle in the 1950s and 1960s. In the book, "*Where Main Street Meets the River*," he tells of his getting fired from his newspaper job. His boss wrote him stating that though he had some good qualities, he would never make a newspaper man and that he ought not to waste any time getting into another business.

Though it was a terrible blow at the time (he had been married only five months), he wrote, looking back on the experience of receiving the dismissal letter, "His letter was the most helpful I ever received."

There Are Some Hard and Tough Things in Life

There are some hard and tough things in life.
Perhaps it is a wonder that there are not more people
Who tear apart in face of them.

There are so many jagged edges.
So many rusty nails sticking up,
So many broken planks
Hanging at head level,
So many loose bricks
That may fall at any minute.
Even by being careful
One does not miss all the rough spots.

When God made man and woman,
He created the human spirit
In God's own image.
Could it be that this is why humans are so tough?
Perhaps people expect to be hurt,
And perhaps they expect also
To go on doing their God-given tasks.
At least it is a fact that we get hurt.
It is also a fact that many tough spirits
Do not just sit around nursing their hurts,
But by something God has put in us,
Or gives us when we have been hurt,
We go on to our work,
Usually with a new and deeper feeling,
And sometimes with a limp.

JULY 10, 1968

My Burden

It is a dark brown color
Thicker at some places than at others,
But dull and heavy withal.
There are not many bright spots in it.
Occasionally there is a flicker of light
That gets to me through it.
But it is dull and heavy.
Whether it can ever be dissolved or removed,
I do not really know.

Perhaps if I could get it moved about,
So that it is not just an indescribable mass,
But carefully molded, as if by hand,
Into the shape of a cross,
Maybe then it could be borne.

OCTOBER 6, 1967

Whistling or Crying

In the 1920s, life on the farm in Mississippi was not easy. It was especially difficult for people who were sharecroppers. On our farm there was the Clarence Watson family of sharecroppers. Clarence was a smallish man, and his wife was much larger and stronger. They had a number of children, and we always suspected that Clarence's wife tried to keep him in line, even if it took force to do so. Clarence milked the cows for us early every morning. We would often hear him coming across the field to get the milk buckets to go to the barn and milk. He would be whistling. As a young teenager, one day I said to him, knowing something of how difficult life was for him, "Clarence, why do you whistle when you come to work?" Clarence said, "I whistle to keep from crying."

Trials

Be like the promontory against which the waves continually break, but it stands firm and tames the fury of the water around it. Unhappy am I, because this has happened to me? Not so, but happy am I, though this has happened to me, because I continue free from pain, neither crushed by the present nor fearing the future. For such a thing as this might have happened to every man, but every man would not have continued free from pain on such an occasion.

—MARCUS AURELIUS

Separation, Longing, and Prayer

In my experience nothing tortures us so much as longing . . . . When we are forcibly separated from those we love, we simply cannot, like so many others, contrive for ourselves some cheap substitute elsewhere—I don't mean because of moral considerations, but because we are what we are . . . . All we can do is to wait patiently; we must suffer the unutterable agony of separation, and feel the longing until it makes us sick. For that is the only way in which we can preserve our relationship with our loved ones unimpaired. There have been a few occasions in my life when I have had to learn what homesickness means. There is no agony worse than this, and during these months in prison I have sometimes been terribly homesick. And as I am sure you will have to go through the same agony during these coming months, I wanted to tell what I had learnt from it in case it may be of some help to you. The first invariable effect of such longing is an itching desire to abandon the daily routine, with the result that our lives become disordered. I used to be tempted to stay in bed after six in the morning ...and to sleep on. Up to now I have never succumbed to that temptation. I realized that that would have been the first stage of capitulation, and no doubt worse would have followed . . . . Another point, I am sure it is best not to talk to strangers about our feelings; that only makes matters worse, though we should always be ready to listen to the troubles of others. Above all, we must never give way to self-pity . . . .

We must simply hold out and win through. That sounds very hard at first, but at the same time it is a great consolation, since leaving the gap unfilled preserves the bonds between us. It is nonsense to say that God fills the gap; he does not fill it, but keeps it empty so that our communion with another may be kept alive, even at the cost of pain . . . . The dearer and richer our memories, the more difficult the separation. But gratitude converts the pangs of memory into tranquil joy. The beauties of the past are not endured as a thorn in the flesh, but as a gift precious for its sake. We must not wallow in our memories or surrender to them, just as we don't gaze all the time as at a valuable present, but get it out from time to time, and for the rest hide it away as a treasure we know is there all the time . . . . It has been borne in upon me here with peculiar force that a concrete situation can always be mastered, and that only fear and anxiety magnify them to an immeasurable degree beforehand. From the moment we awake until we fall asleep we must commend our loved ones wholly and unreservedly to God, and leave them in his hands, transforming our anxiety for them into prayers on their behalf.

—DIETRICH BONHOEFFER

Christ Is In the World

In the world of persistent darkness,
    Christ penetrates with an unquenchable light.

In the world of varied hates,
    Christ demonstrates an invariable love.

In the world of violent deaths,
    Christ died on the violent cross to redeem.

In the world of sorrowful separation,
    Christ offers a fellowship that death cannot break.

In the world where people are selfishly exclusive,
    Christ offers a table where all are welcome.

In the world of painful hunger,
    Christ offers physical and spiritual bread.

In the world where many cannot find their place,
    Christ says, "I go to prepare a place for you."

In the world where there may be no tomorrows,
    Christ says, "Today, when you hear my voice—Come!"

OCTOBER 2, 1969

When the Faith of the Church Is There

The church is the place where God and human being meet
in the deepest experiences of life.

- When tragedy strikes, the faith of the Church is there.

- When cancer eats away at the body until it can function no
  more, the faith of the Church is there.

- When a baby or child's life is taken and reason has no
  answer, the faith of the Church is there.

- When a young person seeks to sort out the meaning
  and purpose of life, the faith of the Church is there.

- When sinning brings guilt that hangs heavy and forgiveness
  is sought, the faith of the Church is there.

- When old age has a person coming face to face with life's
  end, the faith of the Church is there.

- When love and dreams die and marriages and families are
  torn apart, the faith of the Church is there.

- When Isolation and loneliness bring their heavy dark cloud,
  the faith of the Church is there.

- When answers are sought to the deep unexplainable
  questions of life that produce and agonizing "Why," the faith
  of the Church is there.

There will always be issues, but where people meet God in the
deepest experiences of life, there is where the soul of the
Church is.

(From a sermon preached at the First Presbyterian Church in Anniston,
Alabama on Sunday, September 14, 2003)

The Home Inside Ourselves

There *is* no place like home.
Home is our castle.
The American Bill of Rights
Recognizes the home as inviolate.

When the slings and arrows of life come,
Then our home is our refuge.
There we can find solace,
Our wounds can be bound up,
Our spirits can be revived,
And we can find comfort and peace.
There is sanctity about the home.
From the home strength is drawn
To meet the challenges of living
In a world that is turbulent and stressful.

Once when a man broke
Under the pressures of life
And made an end of it all,
His friend said,
"He had no private home inside himself.
So when troubles forced him home,
He had nowhere to go."

(Thoughts stirred by Frederick Buechner)

SEPTEMBER 21, 2009

The Emergency Room for the Soul

There are times when we need to go to an emergency room.
There has been a wreck and the body has been injured.
The heart has an irregular beat. A fever is out of control.
There is unexplained bleeding. A severe pain has developed.
The reasons to go to an emergency room are multiple.
A chapel is an emergency room for the soul.
The reasons for the soul's need of an emergency room are multiple.
A teenager is adrift.
In the silence of the chapel something deep within is reached.
There has been a death in the family.
The grief is overwhelming.
In the silence of the chapel the edge of comfort is felt.
A broken marriage has left deep gashes in the spirit.
In the silence of the chapel, hope seeps into the places that hurt.
The souls needs for an emergency room are many.
Why is a chapel an emergency room for the soul?
In the silence God is there.
The human voices are quieted
And the souls own voice becomes quiet.
And the reality of God who no one has ever seen
Begins to heal our brokenness and soothe our hurts.
We leave the chapel with quietness in our spirit.
In the mystery of God's love
Something down deep has been touched.

(Thoughts stirred by an article, "A Chapel is Where You Can Hear Something
Beating Below Your Heart," by Pico Iyer)

APRIL 16, 2012

They Were Tough

My mother. She gave birth to three children.
After the birth of the third child,
The vicious disease of cancer appeared.
In the early years the treatment was severe.
She endured the agonies of radium.
All this time there was the growing awareness
That an early death would take her
From her little children,
Ages ten months, two years, and three years old.
This was a mother's two-fold agony.

My father. Not a third time!
His first wife gave birth to three children,
And then she died.
His second wife gave birth to three children,
And then she died.
His third wife gave birth to three children,
And now she was going to die from cancer.

I cannot imagine his struggle to cope.
Heavy questions surely sprang up in his mind
And grew to maturity without being answered.

The setting for this real life drama
Was the harsh and crude pattern of life
In rural Mississippi in the teens and twenties
Of the twentieth century.
No electricity. No running water. No indoor plumbing.
No telephones. No super markets. Wood stoves for cooking.
Fireplaces for warmth from the winter's cold.
No escape from Mississippi's summer heat.
Few effective medicines. Money was scarce.
No luxuries.
My mother and father were tough.

Adversities

Now at age ninety, thoroughly immersed in a life
Filled with all the necessities and an abundance of luxuries,
I have a new and deeper sense
of gratitude and admiration for my mother and father.
What they have given me far exceeds
Any tangible things which they did not have to give.

I have known these things since childhood,
But now I feel the impact of their toughness.
My rich blessings in life are rooted
In the gift from my father and mother.

(The day before Thanksgiving and 146 years after the date of
my father's birth)

NOVEMBER 23, 2011

Part 7

Challenges

Challenges and Responses

How do civilizations come into being? Not by climate, soil, or situation favoring the process; on the contrary, by overcoming obstacles . . . .

The author (Arnold Toynbee) proceeds to examine these adverse conditions at length under a number of headings: hard countries, blows, pressures, penalizations. Challenge and Response is the formula in which he summarizes this movement in human history, a rhythm which makes itself felt over the entire field of human action.

— PIETER GAYL

The Ups and Downs of Life

We are human, and we all have our ups and downs.

There are times:
  When the road seems dreary and endless;
  The skies seem grey and threatening;
  Music has gone out of our lives;
  Loneliness has engulfed us;
  Courage has seeped out of our spirits.

God's love is from everlasting to everlasting,
And with the faith that this is true,
We are blessed by praying:
  Flood the road we travel with light;
  Turn our eyes to see where the skies are full of promise;
  Tune our ears to hear again the music of joy;
  Strengthen our sense of comradeship with past travelers;
  Stir our failing courage with the memory of brave hearts.

So with enlivened spirits,
We may live victoriously
Through all the ups and downs of life.

(Thoughts stirred by the prayers of E.B. Pusey, selected by Mary Wilder Tileston)

NOVEMBER 28, 2007

Make No Little Plans

Make no little plans.
Little plans have no power to stir men's souls,
And if realized have no power to bring satisfaction.

—DANIEL BURNHAM

When God Seems Absent

Job had many problems:
Loss of possessions, family, and health.
He had another problem:
He could not get in touch with God.
He said, "I go forward and backward,
I go to the left and to the right,
But I cannot perceive him."

So what does Job do?
How does he handle this feeling
That he cannot get in touch with God?
He concludes that even though
He cannot see or perceive God,
Yet God sees him,
And knows what he is experiencing.
That enables him to hold on
And ultimately come through the fire as gold.

O Lord,
   When the way of life seems hard,
   And the brightness of life is gone,
   Give us the wisdom
      That deepens faith when sight is dim,
      That enlarges trust when understanding
         Is not clear.

OCTOBER 19, 2007

The Pine at Timberline

Up the mountain trail the walker went.
Up and up until the timberline was reached.
There it was, the timberline pine.
The gnarled and twisted trunk
Had stood against each storm
Of wind and fury and icy cold.
Its tenuous deep rooted grip
Had held it there at crag's edge.

Today it stands in the golden
Light of the shining sun.
A gentle breeze moves the twigs and needles
As if to say, "Here I am."
The cold wind and freezing rain,
The jagged lightening flashes,
And the harsh claps of thunder
Have passed, leaving quiet and peace
In the warming sun and refreshing breeze.

But it's gnarled and twisted trunk
And its tenacious roots clinging
To the rocky earth tell us
That there have been storms.
The timberline pine stands peacefully
On the side of the mountain.
But storms will come again,
And the rugged timberline pine will survive.

And the walker has been given a lesson.

(Thoughts stirred by "A Mountaintop" by Morton T. Kelsey)

OCTOBER 2, 2006

The Power of Solid Hope

Our lives are filled with superficial expressions of hope.
I hope it will rain tomorrow.
I hope it will be a sunny day tomorrow.
I hope we will win the game.
I hope we can get there before night.
I hope the plane is on time.
I hope I will feel better tomorrow.
We but touch the fringes of hope
In these superficial expressions.

When hard realities of life bring fear,
When the pain of suffering is intense,
When worry becomes deep and heavy,
When uncertainty weakens our foundations,
And then we are given the gift of hope
Which is laced with faith
And is infused with a belief
In the love and goodness of God.
Then we will have entered
Into the essence of solid hope
From which the human spirit
Can draw strength and power.

(Thoughts stirred by the words of Savonarola from Prison,
in a meditation on Psalm 31)

SEPTEMBER 7, 2006

Solid Footing for the Spirit

In my youth I worked one summer
On the building of a large dam
That created Sardis Lake in Mississippi.
We carried heavy metal cylinders on our shoulders
Up the side of the soft sandy dam.
It was much harder to carry them
On the unstable footing
Than carrying them on solid ground.

A heavy load can be more easily carried
When there is solid footing.
Solid footing for the spirit?
By faith to know that God is love,
That I do not carry my load alone,
That God infuses the human spirit
With some of the qualities of eternity,
This is footing for the spirit
That makes the load more easily carried.

JULY 20, 2006

Advancing Years

Our years have always been advancing,
But now year has been added to year,
And each new year brings new challenges.

One whose years numbered ninety, prayed,
"I come to thee for help to meet
The trials of *advancing years*."

Then specifics followed:
    Give me courage and patience
        To bear infirmities, privations, and loneliness.
    Help me to fight temptations
        To be exacting, selfish, unreasonable,
        Irritable, and complaining.
    Preserve my mental faculties
        Unimpaired to the end.
    Keep my heart and affections warm
        That I may never fail to sympathize
        With the joys, sorrows, and interests of others.
    Make me to be deeply grateful
        For the love and forbearance of those around me.
    Fit and prepare me against the hour of death,
        That I may face it fearlessly,
        Trusting in thy promise to be with me
        As I pass through the dark valley.
    Let me depart in peace
        Knowing my soul will be received
        Into thine everlasting kingdom.

    Thanks be unto my Lord and Savior
        Jesus Christ.
        Amen.

(Paraphrase of an ancient prayer by Alethea L. Grenfell, aged ninety,
selected by Mary Wilder Tileston)

SEPTEMBER 21, 2007

Toward Perfection

"March on. Do not tarry.
To go forward is to move toward perfection.
March on, and fear not the thorns
Or the sharp stones on life's path."*

Toward perfection is the word.
No one ever reaches perfection.
If someone thinks he is perfect,
He deludes himself.
Nobody else thinks he is perfect.

There are thorns,
But some thorny bushes have roses.
Pause and see the beauty of the roses
And smell their sweet fragrance.

There are sharp stones.
Do what Leila said:
"Watch where you puts your foots."

Do not stop or tarry,
Because of thorns and sharp stones.
March on! *Toward* perfection!

*From *Secrets of the Heart* by Kahlil Gebran

JUNE 24, 2008

Good Days

At this stage of life, what makes good days?
Beautiful days in fall, winter, spring, and summer.
Little things like the color of autumn leaves,
The warm fire when it is cold outside,
The early flowers in the spring,
And the glorious colors of the azaleas.
But somehow those are extras.

There are some things basic to good days.
To experience life as a gift of God.
To feel the exuberance of a healthy body.
To have deep relationships of love and trust
So as not to be torn or consumed
By the tensions and strains of conflict.
To have a sense of self worth,
But being way short of conceit or arrogance.
The freedom to go or come and say yes or no.
To feel that your life still has meaning and purpose.
To have enough of this world's goods
Not to be anxious or worried
About the basic physical necessities of life.

We have much to do with whether or not
We have these basics of good days,
But we must never forget
That we are not totally in charge.
We do our best, but there is providence over us.
We are fortunate if our good days;
Strengthen us for the days that are not so good,
Because it is true:
    "Into each life some rain must fall,
    Some days must be dark and dreary."*

* (Longfellow)

SEPTEMBER 12, 1995

Part 8

Character

The Goodness of Humanity

As I look over a year of time, I am astonished at the amount of goodness which I have seen, more than I am at anything besides. The evil lies atop, it is in sight of all men (people) who open their eyes, while deeper down there is laid the solid goodness of mankind, which is not always visible, and never at a glance.

—THEODORE PARKER.

Christian Nobility

Think of the report of a wounded Union soldier on the con-
duct of General Robert Lee after the battle of Gettysburg. Lying in a ditch by the roadside, the young soldier discovered
that the General, passing by in retreat, had dismounted from
old Traveler and was coming toward him. "My only thought
was that he meant to kill me. But he looked down at me with
such a sad expression on his face that all fear left me, and I
wondered what he was about. Then he extended his hand to
me, and looked right into my eyes and said, 'My son, I hope
you will soon be well.' After some more words of comfort, he
mounted his horse and went on. If I live a thousand years, I
shall never forget the expression on the General's face. There
he was, retiring from a field that had cost him and his almost
their last hope stopping to say words like that to a man who
had fought him. I cried myself to sleep there upon the bloody
ground."

— WILLIAM CROWE

Success

There is no honest and true work, carried along with
constant and sincere purpose, that ever really fails. If it sometime
seems to be wasted effort, it will prove to us a new lesson of
"how" to walk; the secret of our failures will prove to us the
inspiration of possible successes. Man, living with the highest aims
as best he can, in continuous harmony with them, is a success, no
matter what statistics of failure a near-sighted and half-blind world
of critics and commentators may lay at his door.

High ideals, noble efforts will make seeming failures but trifles;
they need not dishearten us but should prove sources of new strength.
The rocky way may prove safer than the slippery path of smoothness.
Birds cannot fly best with the wind, but against it;
Ships do not progress in calm when the sails flap idly
against the unstrained masts.

The alchemy of Nature, superior to that of the Paracelsians,
constantly transmute the baser metal of failure into the later pure
gold of higher success, if the mind of the worker is kept true,
constant and untiring in the service, and if he has that sublime
courage that defies fate to its worst while he does his best.

—WILLIAM GEORGE JORDAN

Patience—Makrothumia

The basic meaning of *makrothumia* is patience with people. It is the quality of mind and heart which enables a person so to bear with people that their unpleasantness and maliciousness and cruelty will never drive one to despair, that their folly will never drive one to irritation, and that their unloveliness will never alter ones love. Makrothumia is the spirit which never loses patience with, belief in, and hope for people.

Paul uses this word as he prays that the Christian may

be such that no circumstances can defeat his strength, and no human being defeat his love. He prays for that spirit which will never despair about any situation or person, which will refuse to grow hopeless either about things or people. The Christians fortitude in events and patience with people must be indestructible.

(AUTHOR UNKNOWN)

Fortitude—Hupomene

Hupomone is sometimes translated as patience, but
it does not mean patience in the sense of sitting down
and bearing things, and of simply bowing the head
and letting the tide of events flow over one. It means
not only the ability to bear things, but the ability, in
bearing them, to turn them into glory. It is a conquering
patience. It is the spirit which no circumstance in life
can ever defeat, and which no event can ever vanquish.
It is the ability to deal triumphantly with anything
that life can do to us.

Paul uses this word as he prays that the Christian may

be such that no circumstances can defeat his strength,
and no human being defeat his love. He prays for that
spirit which will never despair about any situation or
person, which will refuse to grow hopeless either about
things or people. The Christian's fortitude in events
and patience with people must be indestructible.

(AUTHOR UNKNOWN)

One by One

In Exodus 23:29,30, God, through Moses, is telling the Jewish people certain laws of human society to follow, and at the same time promising that he will drive out the enemies of the land so that it shall be theirs. But the way it is to be done is significant. They will not be driven out all at one year, lest the land be empty and the wild beasts multiply. But they shall be driven out little by little until you are increased and possess the land. But it is important that during that time they make no compromise with the enemies or worship their gods.

So it is in this way that sin is taken out of our lives. Thomas A Kempis said something about—you are doing well if you get rid of one vice a year.

—JAMES S. STEWART

A Deeper Level

Like hit-and-run drivers, we injure our souls by the speed with which we move on the surface; and then we rush away, leaving our bleeding souls alone. We miss, therefore, our depth and our true life. And it is only when the picture that we have of ourselves breaks down completely, only when we had derived from that picture, and only when an earthquake shakes and disrupts the surface of our self-knowledge, that we are willing to look into a deeper level of our being.

—PAUL TILLICH

Integrity

Charles Kingsley in a letter to his wife when his forthright teaching and preaching involved him in a turmoil of bitter controversy and strife and when friends and relatives pleaded with him to "put the tongue of discretion in the cheek of propriety," wrote:

"I will not be a liar. I will speak in season and out of season. I will not take council with flesh and blood, and flatter myself with the dream that, while every man on earth back to Abel who ever tried to testify against the world has been laughed at, misunderstood, slandered, and that—bitterest of all—by the very people he loved. Am I alone to escape. My faith is clear and I will follow in it. He who died for me and who gave me you, shall I not trust him through whatever new and strange paths he may lead me?"

— ROBERT J. MCCRACKEN

Inward Liberty

If thou intend and seek nothing else but the will of God and the good of thy neighbor, thou shalt thoroughly enjoy inward liberty.

—THOMAS A KEMPIS

The Right Thing

There is always a voice saying the right thing to you somewhere, if only you will listen for it.

—THOMAS HUGHES

Conscience and Remorse

"Goodbye," I said to my conscience.
"Goodbye for aye and aye."
And I put her hands off harshly
And turned my face away.
And conscience smitten sorely,
Returned not from that day.

But a time came when my spirit
Grew weary of its pace.
I cried, "Come back my conscience,
I long to see thy face."
But conscience answered, "I cannot,
Remorse sits in my place."

(From Dunbar, *World's Great Library of Literature*)

Courage

Wonder walks all the way
with a person of courage.

—HAROLD CASE

Taking Risk in Doing Good

I was asked to accept the situation of one of the son's curators and trusted to clear out his affairs and hers—at least I will not fail for want of application. I have lent her L300 on a second loan (and therefore doubtful) security over her house in Newington, bought for £1000 and on which L600 is already secured. I have no connection with the family except that of compassion, and may not be rewarded even by thanks when the young man comes of age. I have known my father often so treated by those which he had labored to serve. But if we do not run some hazard in our attempts to do good, where is the merit of them?

—SIR WALTER SCOTT'S JOURNAL

Scrap Iron

Scrap iron has one quality:
It is tough!
Heavy blows do not break it.
Heat does not melt it.
Cold does not freeze it.
Time does not deteriorate it.
In the end it is still there.

For over fifty years I have watched you.
You are tough!
When heavy blows come, they do not break you.
When the heat is on, you do not melt.
When harsh cold comes, you do not freeze.
As time passes, you do not deteriorate.
Through all the hardships that have come,
You are there: tough and strong.
That is why with admiration and pride
I call you: My Scrap Iron Daughter.

OCTOBER 22, 2006

Part 9

Grace/Forgiveness

The Two All-Determining Facts of Life

"Moreover the law entered, that the offence might abound. But where sin abounded, grace did much more abound."

—ROMANS 5:20

These words of Paul summarize his apostolic experience, his religious message as a whole, and the Christian understanding of life. To discuss these words, or to make them the text of even several sermons, has always seemed impossible to me. I have never dared to use them before. But something has driven me to consider them during the past few months, a desire to give witness to the two facts which appeared to me, in hours of retrospection, as the all-determining facts of our life: The abounding of sin and the greater abounding of grace.

—PAUL TILLICH

Traders in the Temple
Or
Merchants in the Church

Jesus went into the temple
And cast out those who bought and sold.
Do we go to Church to buy and sell?

Do we bring our good works, our offerings,
Our prayers, our moral and ethical behavior
And lay them before God
In the hope that God
Will give us something in return?
Merchants sell to get something in return.

There is no way we can obligate God.
God is unbound and free
And acts out of pure love.
That is the meaning of grace.

(Thoughts stirred by reading from Eckhart's sermon
on Matt.21:12, August 13, 2006)

Gratitude

The garden was covered with a light snow,
And the full moon cast its brilliant glow.
An unseen bird gave forth its clear song.
The soft white snow will not last long.
The moon will wax and wane.
And the wonders of nature will be the same,
As the centuries come and go.
Other birds will sing as though
By song they would say,
We praise our God this day.
And human beings made in the image of God
Look out on the world and with a nod
Affirm that God is good and faithful,
And pray that we may always be grateful.

FEBRUARY 13, 2006

The Running Father

The story is told of a Chinese artist who undertook to paint this story. His first attempt showed the father standing, waiting at the gate for his son who was seen approaching in the distance. When the artist showed his picture to a Christian friend, his friend exclaimed, "Oh, no, you don't have it right. The father shouldn't be standing, waiting. He should be running to meet his son."

"But no Chinese father could do that!" said the artist.

"That is just the point," replied his friend. "No human father would, but this is the astonishing story of a father that tells us about God's amazing love! He loves us like that."

"I see," replied the artist.

The next picture he painted showed the father running to meet his son, and in his hurry, he had put on shoes that didn't match.

—REUEL HOWE

Our Imperfect Lives

The little son with his own hands
Makes a gift for his father.
He takes his box of crayons
And carefully colors a picture.
He uses yellow, red, blue and green
And tries to stay in the lines.
As he gives it to his father,
His eyes radiate his childish love.

The father takes the picture
And sees that the colors
Are not always within the lines.
The colors run together here and there.
It is not a perfect picture.
But the loving father
Puts his arm around his son
And holds him tight and says,
"What a beautiful picture, my son."

"Thou shall love the Lord thy God,
With all thine heart, with all thy soul,
And with all thy might,"
Is the command of the law of God.
Try as we may no human being
Can perfectly fulfill this commandment.

But when the gift of an imperfect life
Is offered up to the heavenly Father,
God opens his arms
And warmly declares his love for us,
And accepts the gift of our imperfect lives.

(Thoughts stirred by readings from John Calvin's Institutes
about human imperfection and God's accepting love)

OCTOBER 4, 2006

The Absence of Grace

For whether I have with me good men, either religious brethren, or faithful friends; whether holy books or beautiful treatises, or sweet psalms and hymns; all these help but little, and have but little savor, when grace forsaketh me, and I am left in mine own poverty.

At such time there is no better remedy than patience, and the denying of myself according to the will of God.

I never found any so religious and devout, that he had not sometimes a withdrawing of grace, or felt not some decrease of zeal.

—THOMAS A KEMPIS

God's Gift at Dawn

Some nights are dark.
The mists of darkness have
Enveloped the world.
There is no soft moonlight,
No sparkle of starlight.
In the deep darkness there is silence.
Though time is surely moving,
Nothing marks its slow progress.
In the dark cold winter night,
Everything seems frozen into still life.

Then softly and quietly and slowly
A gentle and almost imperceptible light
Begins to spread, and as it does,
It pushes back the all pervasive darkness.
Its coming makes no sound.
But then as a special gift of a thoughtful God,
There is the crystal clear singing
Of a single bird who seems to know
That the darkness is disappearing
And a wonderful new day is dawning.

FEBRUARY 11, 2006

On a Clear Day

On a clear day
The eyes can see
The blue sky,
The green grass,
The rustling of the leaves,
The rippling of the stream,
The majesty of the mountains.
And it is good.

On a clear and quiet day
The eyes of the soul
Can see into forever,
The songs of angels,
The beauty of peace,
The fullness of joy,
The whisper of love.
And it is good.

MAY 13, 2006

Forgive?

This is part of a conversation
between General Oglethorpe and John Wesley:

General Oglethorpe: "I never forgive."

John Wesley: "Then may you never sin."

AUGUST 13, 2006

Heart and Spirit

Along the way with the ups and downs of human life
The heart becomes unclean
And the right spirit becomes the wrong spirit.
So there is the need to often repeat the prayer:
Create in me a clean heart and renew a right spirit.
The strains and stresses of life
And the unhappy relationships that sometime develop
May cause envy, jealousy, anger, and even bitterness.
Such barnacles attach to our spirit,
And penetrate our hearts.

Each new day there is the need to pray:
Create in me a clean heart and renew a right spirit.
God can create and recreate a clean heart
And renew and renew a right spirit,
And we can keep trying to keep our hearts clean
And keep a right spirit within us.
But again and again there will be the need to be
The cleaning of the heart
And the renewing of the right spirit.

APRIL 3, 2007

Part 10

History

The Most Recent Significant Event in History

Arnold Toynbee has been developing the idea that the secular civilization called "Western civilization" is not the most important development of this age because civilizations rise and fall while Christianity, being the high religion, is of more significance. He writes:

The greatest new event will then not be the monotonous rise of yet another secular civilization out of the bosom of the Christian Church in the course of these latter centuries; it will still be the Crucifixion and its spiritual consequences. There is one curious result of our immense modern scientific discoveries which is, I think, often overlooked. On the vastly changed time-scale which our astronomers and geologists have opened up to us, the beginning of the Christian era is an extremely recent date; on a time-table in which nineteen hundred years are no more than the twinkling of an eye, the beginning of the Christian era is only yesterday. It is only on the old-fashioned time-scale, on which the creation of the world and the beginning of life on the planet were reckoned to have taken place not more that six thousand years ago, that a span of nineteen hundred years seems a long period of time and the beginning of the Christian era therefore seems a far-off event. In fact it is a very recent event—perhaps the most recent significant event in history—and that brings us to a consideration of the prospects of Christianity in the future history of mankind on Earth.

—ARNOLD TOYNBEE

The Time to Live

"History is turning a corner,
And is about to enter upon something new,"
Spoke the brilliant seer and the perceptive prophet.

I have become familiar
With the way it looks and feels
As I walk the street beside this wall.
I haven't been around the corner,
And I do not know how it will be.
But if it is history turning a corner,
That means that no one else
Has turned this corner either.

There's got to be some excitement
About turning a corner with history!
Of Jesus it was said,
"He lifted empires off their hinges
And turned the course of history
Out of its channel."
Perhaps He is doing it again,
And in our time!
When God has history turning corners,
It is an exciting time to live!

MAY 13, 1971

Christianity in the Second and Third Centuries

Toynbee says that there were three secrets of the coming success of religion (Christianity was one of them.) in the 2nd and 3rd centuries, A.D., as a reaction to the military, political, and economic offensive of the Graeco-Roman civilization:

1. The weariness of the clash of cultures.
2. They present a fraternity which overcomes the clashes of cultures.
3. They bring "human members into a saving fellowship with a superhuman being . . . in the presence of divinities to whom we can devote ourselves with all our heart and mind and strength." This is after being disillusioned by the "deified militarist" whom Toynbee calls a "flagrant scandal," that is Alexander the Great, and by the "deified policeman," that is Augustus Caesar, whom he says liquidated his fellow gangsters.

— ARNOLD TOYNBEE

Part 11

Social Change

The Age of Revolution

If there is any period one would desire to be born in, is it not the age of Revolution; when the old and the new stand side by side, and admit of being compared; when the energies of all men are searched by fear and by hope; when the historic glories of the old, can be compensated by the rich possibilities of the new era? This time, like all times, is a very good one, if we but know what to do with it.

—Ralph Waldo Emerson,
an address to the Phi Beta Kappa Society
at Harvard University in August, 1837.

The Central Aim of Social Change

What we will tell them will be simply this: "Whether you are revolutionaries or restorers of order (according to historical circumstances) remember always that your aim must be to seek the welfare of man, human freedom, human dignity, man's participation in the human enterprise, and man's responsibility for controlling it. Everything else is merely words and romanticism."

—ROGER MAHL

Disturbing Light

At a meeting of the Synod of the Southeast, Malcolm Calhoun stood to give a Church and Society report. Behind the speaker's stand was a window with venetian blinds that were partially open. The light coming through shined directly in the eyes of the listeners. Someone got up and asked that the venetian blind be closed because the light in their eyes bothered them. The venetian blind cord was broken, but a movie screen was attached above the window, and it was pulled down over the window.

Malcolm Calhoun who was going to present a controversial report on race relations began by saying, "The light sometimes gets in our eyes and bothers us. Sometimes when the light of God gets in our eyes it bothers us too." Then he proceeded to speak of the application of the light of God to our relations to our fellow man.

The Word of the Gospel

It was 1963. The Civil Rights Revolution was in full swing. Birmingham and Selma were blowing apart. Anniston, Alabama was in turmoil. The Freedom Riders Bus had been burned in Anniston. Two members of the Anniston commission had been courageous enough to appoint a biracial Human Relations Council, the first officially appointed one in Alabama, and maybe the first in the Southeast. Progress had been made in Anniston, but not enough. On Sunday afternoon, September 15, 1963, the Human Relations Council and the Anniston Public Library Board had planned for the library to be integrated by having two African American ministers who were members of the Human Relations Council to go to the library and register, check out some books, and leave. When they got to the library, they were met by a mob of KKK hoodlums and others and attacked with clubs, chains, and knives. The ministers escaped with their lives, but were severely beaten. That night the mayor and another City Commissioner, the Library Board Chairman, and myself, the Chairman of the Biracial Human Relations Council, went to the home of the minister who had been most badly beaten to express our concern and support. The other minister who had not been as badly hurt as the other minister was there. In talking about the situation I asked what the reaction of the black community was. He said they had a mass meeting at the Seventeenth Street Baptist Church and that he had preached. I asked this twenty-four year old Methodist Minister how he could preach after being attacked by a white mob that afternoon. I will never forget the way he looked at me and said, "Phil, the word of the gospel had to be spoken tonight." It saved the Anniston community from a blood bath that night.

1960—Change—2007

I worshipped at Church this morning.
Thanksgiving is almost here
And hymns of gratitude were sung.
Not new ones, but old traditional ones.
The robed choir processed with dignity.
Two sprays of fall colored flowers appropriately
Marked the season and warmed the sanctuary.
The minister in his black Geneva robe
Spoke of God and God's gifts
That called for a response of gratitude.
This was good and meaningful worship
As it has occurred in Churches
In cities and towns throughout America
For several hundred years.

Today, as every Sunday,
There was the time when little children
Came to the front of the Sanctuary
And sat on the floor as a leader
Spoke to them in appropriate words for children.
The little boys squirmed
Or sat with their elbows on their knees
And their heads in their hands.
The little girls all carefully dressed
Smiled and sometimes quietly giggled.

I noticed one little girl dressed
In a soft purple dress
And well polished white shoes.
Her hair was tied up on top
With a matching purple ribbon.
And she quietly sat
Surrounded by other little girls and boys.
She was a beautiful little black child,

And it all seemed so easy and natural.
Change! Good Change!

NOVEMBER 18, 2007

The Powerful Image

Will was a fragile boy ten years old.
He had no sisters or brothers.
He was an only child
Greatly loved by a father and mother.

He grew up in the old South
Where whites were whites
And blacks were blacks
In a world together, but far apart.

Suddenly his world was shattered.
His farm manager father suddenly died
In the cotton fields
Surrounded by black field workers.

They carefully put his body on the soft hay
On a wagon pulled by two mules.
Will's boyish eyes saw his ashen father
And looked at his devastated mother.

Sensitive spirit that he was
He observed in depth the burial events.
The lowering of the casket into the grave
By two ropes held by black hands.

The red Alabama clay was to fill the grave.
The rural tradition was that the men in the family
Quietly and carefully shoveled the dirt on the coffin
As a last symbol of love and devotion.

As the men in the family stepped forward
And grasped the handles of shovels
A rough and knarled black hand
Touched the white man's shoulder.

And with dignity and compassion
In soft tones of the black southern dialect
A voice would say words forever set in Will's mind:
"We would like to do that!"

There was the sound of the first shovel of dirt
Dropping on the casket
Breaking the heavy silence
That surrounds the presence of death.

Then black hands added more shoveled clay
As the tears from black eyes
Mingled with the drops of sweat
Until there was a rounded mound of clay.

Thirty years later ten year old Will
Has reached maturity and is pastor
Of a Presbyterian Church
Set in the deep Alabama culture.

The black people are moving at last.
They want to be free from the discrimination
Of a vicious segregated society.
They would come knocking on the door of the Church.

What would the Church do?
What would Will do?
While white southerners said,
"You cannot enter here,"

Will saw in those at the Church doors
The black hands that had shoveled the dirt
To fill his father's grave
And the solemn tear-stained faces,

And he heard in their voices
The echo of words long since
Carved into his mind forever:
"We would like to do that."

Strengthened and emboldened and cleansed
By the power of that image,
Will entered the pulpit and declared:
"In God's name, they are welcome here!"

An image so personal and so secret
Had been in his mind undisclosed
For thirty years and was made known
In his sermon: A Sermon in Clay.

That image was the secret
Of his sense of fairness and justice,
The stimulus for his compassion
For a downtrodden race of people.
Timid as he was by nature,
This image made him courageous and strong
To declare the justice and love of God
For all of God's people.

(Written to be read at the burial service of J. Will Ormond at Old Side
Cemetery, Bethel Presbyterian Church, April 27, 2006)

MARCH 29, 2006

The Dove Flies On

A dove of peace.
He flew to his people.
His people in turn
Provided a branch
On which he came to roost.
Now he is gone,
But the dove flies on.*

As the waters of the great flood receded,
Noah released a dove.
It flew away over the waters,
But finding no place to stop and rest
It returned to the ark.
Sometime later Noah released the dove again.
It returned with a green olive leaf in its bill.
Once again Noah released the dove.
This time the dove did not return.
It found branches in which to roost.

Today the dove of peace
Flies over the world's troubled waters.
It searches for branches on the trees of the world
Where it can stop and rest.
Occasionally there is a branch
That rises above the troubled waters,
And when the branch is cut down,
The dove flies on . . . .

*A reference to Martin Luther King written by Adam Engles Kirchen
in the seventh grade, from *From Southern Wrongs to Civil Rights*
by Sara Mitchell Parsons

JULY 20, 2009

Part 12

Death/Eternal Life

Missing Light

For sixty-seven years my life was blessed
    by a bright light.
It illumined my way, and its constant brightness
    shone into the dark places.
It gave a pleasant glow to daily life
    and illuminated the way for
my next steps into the unknown future.
    It lit up my senses and made my life
Filled with a deeper sense of life's meaning
    and brought me love, joy, and happiness.

Now that light is gone.
    I am not in total darkness,
But the light has been dimmed.

SEPTEMBER 24, 2012

When Time and Eternity Meet

We each live out our time.
Or another way to say it is,
Our earthly time comes to an end.
At the boundary of our earthly time,
Our eternity begins when time is no more.
The dynamic and everlasting eternity
Which has become ours
Has no need of the tick-tocking
Of the fleeting earthly time
 For time has lost its power to eternity.
No more agony of separation
For God and loved ones will be with us,
And every tear shall be wiped from our eyes.
Death shall be no more,
And neither shall there be mourning,
Nor crying, nor pain,
For the former earthly time
  Has passed away.

(Thoughts stirred by Dietrich Bonhoeffer and the book of Revelation)

NOVEMBER 25, 2012

The Seriousness of Death

Do not deceive yourself about the seriousness of death—not death in general, not the death of somebody else, but your own death—by nice arguments for the immortality of the soul. The Christian message is more realistic than those arguments. It knows that we, *really we*, have to die; it is not just a part of us that has to die. And within Christianity there is only one "argument" against death: the forgiveness of sins, and the victory over him who has the power of death. It speaks of the coming of the eternal to us, becoming temporal in order to restore our eternity.

—PAUL TILLICH

The Fragrance of Eternity

All living beings die!
Only humans smell the fragrance of eternity!

The suffering Job got a whiff of the fragrance,
Therefore he asked out loud:
"If a man die shall he live again?"

The fragrance of eternity
Swirls in the forest air
As in the hope that the tree
That has been cut down
Leaving only a stump,
Will at the scent of water
Bud and put forth branches.*

The scent of the water of life
Is an awakening fragrance
That stirs the soul
To yearn for eternity.

When death is near
Faith puts off an aroma
That is the fragrance of eternity.

Drink deeply of the water of life.
Breathe deeply the aroma in the air.

It is the fragrance of eternity.

*Job 14:7-9

AUGUST 24, 2008

Sorrow's Pattern

When a loved one dies
There is a sharp and penetrating sorrow.

In the days and weeks that follow
Slowly, slowly, the sorrow
Seeps into the whole being.

The loved one is gone. It is really so.
Memories keep coming back.
The sorrow seems to attach
To some of them.
And each time they come
It brings a new wave of sorrow.
The sorrow subsides a bit,
But when the memory returns
So will the sorrow.
But thankfully each time
The wave of sorrow returns
It is less painful.

But there are other memories
Of good and happy times.
These help the sorrows diminish.
There are also other memories.
Memories of the promises of God
That there is life after death.
As the reality of these promises
Seep into our spirit
Its comforting power gradually
Overcomes the sorrow.
As the time stretches out
Through the months,
Slowly, slowly the sorrow
Becomes more bearable.

Death/Eternal Life

Though the sorrow will always be there,
Life can be good again.
We may walk with a limp
But we can live with it.

SEPTEMBER 7, 2013

The Depth of Joy

Eternal joy is the end of the ways of God. This is the message of all religions. The Kingdom of God is peace and joy. This is the message of Christianity. But eternal joy is not to be reached by living on the surface. It is rather attained by breaking through the surface, by penetrating the deep things of ourselves, of our world, and of God. The moment in which we reach the last depth of our lives is the moment in which we can experience the joy that has eternity within it, the hope that cannot be destroyed, and the truth on which life and death are built. For in the depth is truth; and in the depth is hope; and in the depth is joy.

—PAUL TILLICH

On the Way to Easter

The earth throbs with life.
But much of it is hidden still by
The effects of winter. But it will
Burst forth! And shortly now.

The being throbs with life.
Life for some of us may be covered
Over by the darkness and dullness
Of cold and hard days and a long season
Of dormant spirit. If our beings could
Burst forth with vibrant spiritual life
Just as the earth is about to do,
How thrilling such a renewal would be!

God has said in the Old Testament:
    "The desert shall rejoice and blossom as the rose.
    And the parched ground shall become a pool."
God has said in the New Testament:
    "Behold, I make all things new."

Worship the Lord who made heaven and earth!
Be still and know that he is God!
Expose yourself to the warmth of His Son!
And when Easter comes you may be renewed
    Or made new!

MARCH 6, 1969

Accountability

In 1853, Kierkegaard wrote: "I have something on my conscience as a writer. Let me indicate precisely how I feel about it. There is something quite definite I have to say, and I have it so much upon my conscience that (as I feel) I dare not die without having uttered it. For the instant I die and thus leave this world (so as I understand it) I shall in the very same second (so frightfully fast it goes!), in the very same second I shall be infinitely far away, in a different place where still within the same second (frightful speed!) the question will be put to me: 'Hast thou uttered the definite message quite definitely?' And if I have not done so, what then?"

—WALTER LOWRIE,

A Modern Parable of the Rich Fool

There was a man who started out with no education who worked with his father a year in Alabama and made three bales of cotton. He said to his father, "There must be some place where a person can get more in return for his labor. If there is I am going to find it." He took the money he had cleared for himself from the three bales of cotton and went to the railroad ticket office and said, "How far will this take me?" The ticket agent said, "to Shreveport." He went there and realized he needed to know a great deal more before he could do very much. So he tended cattle while he went to a "Normal School." There he was taught three things: penmanship, arithmetic and English. After eight months he had saved a little money and he went to Memphis. There he got a job with a construction company laying brick in the streets. He watched everything that was done. After a few years he launched a company of his own and eventually became one of the very wealthy men in his section of the country. He was married and had children and grandchildren.

In poor health he came to the point of death and was "scared to death." He was known as a man of iron, but he cried sobs of tears and called in two friends who were not members of his family and said to them, "I am going to die, and I am going to hell." The friends tried to console him, but he said, "No, it is true. I have never done anything for anybody!" The friends said, "But you have meant so much to your wife and children." He replied, "No more that I ought to have done. I've never really done anything for anybody."

(As told by my sister who was one of the friends.)

AUGUST 13, 2006

A Grain of Wheat

Take a grain of wheat. I take a thousand grains of
wheat, and I sow them in the earth. What happens?
They die, and if at the expiration of seven days I
should dig them up they would be worthless. But
I leave them in the earth. The seeds die, but they
die as seeds. They take new life as blades. Out of
death issues life. And in three months I look out
upon a field of waving green—a miracle of resurrection.
The dying grain of wheat is a prophecy of immortality.
It tells us that what appears to be the end is really a
beginning.

—P. J. STACKHOUSE

A Grain of Corn

(I Corinthians 15:35–50)

I hold in my hand a grain of yellow corn.
I note its smallish size
And it's dimpled end
And the way it tapers to a small whitish point.
I see in my mind's eye
A beautiful stalk of corn.
It's deep green long and graceful leaves
Blowing in the gentle breezes.
It stands tall, higher than my head.
And all that came from
A little dimpled yellow grain
That I could hold in my hand.

I have never seen a human
Sperm and egg, so small
And hardly visible to the naked eye.
But from them comes
A human body, legs and toes,
Arms and fingers,
A head with ears and a nose,
And a mouth with a tongue inside.
And invisible in it now
Is a capacity that will emerge
To laugh and cry, think and dream,
And all of the wonderful complexity
Of a human being, body and soul.

In time the lifeless human being
Is carefully put into the ground
Like the planted grain of corn.
Then in time or beyond time
There emerges a spiritual body

That may be as different
As the stalk is from the grain of corn
Or the human being is from
The sperm and egg.
It will have properties
That suit it for the spiritual world
We call heaven.
And another miracle:
It will never wear out
Or become old,
And when the earth has vanished
And is no more,
It will be in the presence
Of the eternal God forever.

OCTOBER 19, 2005

Think Continually

Think continually how many physicians are dead after often contracting their eyebrows over the sick; and how many astrologers after predicting with great pretensions the death of others; how many philosophers after endless discourses on death or immortality; how many heroes after killing thousands; and how many tyrants who have used their power over men's lives with terrible insolence as if they were immortal. Pass then through this little space of time conformably to nature, and end thy journey in content, just as an olive falls when it is ripe, blessing nature who produced it, and thanking the tree it grew on.

Be like the promontory against which the waves continually break, but it stands firm and tames the fury of the water around it. Unhappy am I, because this has happened to me?—Not so, but happy am I, though this has happened to me, because I continue free from pain, neither crushed by the present nor fearing the future. For such a thing as this might have to every man; but every man would not have continued free from pain on such an occasion.

(From *Meditations of Marcus Aurelius,*
translated by George Long Press)

These Are the Words for the Trumpet to Blow

Out of the dark and ancient ages past
Comes the question passed from man to man:
"If a man die, shall he live again?"

Out of the bright and living present
Comes the answer passed from man to man:
"Because I live, you too shall live!"

The angel spoke and said, "He is risen!"
"He is risen," Mary said.
"He is risen," said James and John.
"He is risen," said Peter and the Jews.
"He is risen," said Paul and the gentiles.
And now let the whole world give back
The answer the ancients longed to hear:
"He is risen indeed!"

These are the words for the trumpet to blow.
And indeed the trumpet shall blow,
And the dead in Christ shall rise!
    And corruption shall put on incorruption,
    And mortality shall put on immorality,
And death shall be asked,
    Where is thy sting?
And the grave shall be asked,
    Where is thy victory?
And a multitude of joyful voices
Shall answer in unison:
"Thanks be to God
Who giveth us the victory
Through our Lord Jesus Christ."

APRIL 14, 1968

A Life to Come

If God is justice and God is love,
I am certain as it is possible
To be certain of anything
That there is a life to come.

—WILLIAM BARCLAY

Beyond Pure Intellect

C. S. Lewis has been talking about an experience whereby he is thinking of the state of his departed wife as pure intellect—then he says:

"But I mustn't, because I have come to misunderstand a little less completely what a pure intelligence might be, lean over too far. There is also, whatever it means, the resurrection of the body. We cannot understand. The best is perhaps what we understand least."

—C.S. LEWIS

Recognition in Heaven

John Adams, second president of the United States, gave his views of eternal life after the death of Abigail Adams (his wife) in 1818.

Replying to a letter of sympathy from Jefferson, he wrote:

"I know not how to prove, physically, that we shall know each other in a future state; nor does Revelation, as I can find, give us any positive assurance of such felicity. My reasons for believing it, as I do most undoubtedly, are that I cannot conceive such a being as the human, merely to live and die on this earth. If I did not believe in a future state, I should believe in one God . . . , if there be a future state, why should the Almighty dissolve forever the tender ties which unite us so delightfully in this world, and forbid us to see each other in the next."

—BLISS ISELY

Papa's Dream

My father had four wives. His first wife, Vivian, died after having three children. His second wife, Merab, the sister of Vivian, also died after having three children. Then he married my mother, Ida, and she had three children and died. His fourth wife survived him.

In his older years my father often told me of a very vivid dream that he had over and over again. He dreamed that he was crossing over the last river, and as he came out on the other side, Merab came to meet him. In the last hours before he died, he raised both arms as if he was reaching for Merab who was coming to meet him.

I Was Given a Wonderful Gift Tonight

I was given a wonderful dream tonight.
I had a vivid dream,
And in that dream I saw my mother.
She was dressed in a white dress,
And she was beautiful!
Family was all around:
My father, William, and Cary.
At one point a voice said,
"and this is Phillips."
There was a special moment
When she looked at me.
I felt her joy
At seeing her children again,
And a warm and gentle peace
Seeped into my being.
She looked well and strong
With no sign of the ravages
Of suffering from the cruel disease
That took her from this life
At the age of thirty-nine.

It was a dream
That I had never had before
During the past almost eighty eight years.
It was just a dream,
But the dream was a special gift.

JUNE 30, 2009, 2:00 AM

Going Home

I have lived in this house for many years.
From time to time there were repairs
That needed to be made.
All in all it has been a good house,
And I have enjoyed living in it.
But the time will come when I have to leave.
I will quietly go to the front door,
Open it, and walk out,
And gently close the door
So as to disturb others as little as possible.
I am going home.

MAY 28, 2009

For Everlasting Life

"For a small income a long journey is undertaken; for ever-lasting life many will scarce once lift a foot from the ground."

—THOMAS A KEMPIS

Nobody Really Knows

(An Easter Reflection)

Nobody really knows.
Say what they will,
Nobody really knows.

Since the origin of human beings
The ultimate question has been asked.
As each one experiences the passing years
The question seeps into the mind.
Sometimes the hunger for the truth
Causes it to explode in the mind:
"If a man dies shall he live again?"

Writings by people ancient and modern
Probe the possibilities with fear and hope.
There is one certainty:
From ancient Adam and Eve
To present Adams and Eves,
Every human body ceases to be
And returns to dust and ashes.

Faith and faith alone
Inflames the human spirit with hope.
Unnumbered millions have believed in a special reality:
That Jesus Christ rose from the dead.
That infuses substance into faith,
And that faith has peopled heaven
With a multitude that no one can number.

FEBRUARY 3, 2006

Faith for Dying

One of the bravest, most poignant letters ever written tells of the death of Dr. Edward Wilson, Scott's companion in the Antarctic. Scott himself, dying in his tent, was the writer. "If this letter reaches you, Bill and I will have gone out together. We are very near it now, and I should like you to know how splendid he was at the end—everlastingly cheerful and ready to sacrifice himself for others, never a word of blame to me for leading him into this mess. His eyes have a comfortable blue look of hope and his mind is peaceful with the satisfaction of his faith in regarding himself as part of the great scheme of the Almighty. I can do no more to comfort you than to tell you that he died as he lived, a brave, true man, oh. the best of comrades, the staunchest of friends."

Will you think of that—for does not the secret of spiritual victory in the day of sacrifice lie there—"His eyes with a comfortable blue look of hope, and his mind peaceful with his faith that he is part of the great scheme of the Almighty"? It is on that kind of faith—for each and all of us—that everything in the last resort depends, the faith that our own life, with all its difficulties and problems and hard self-denials and defeated hopes, has nevertheless a place in God's great plan, and that even in the most hurting experiences love almighty is in control. Without that faith, life is bound to lead to bitterness. But with it, the sacrifice becomes the signal for the song.

—JAMES S. STEWART

Meeting Eternity

With this present little book, which itself belongs to a bygone time, I conclude the whole authorship, and then as author (not an author simply, but the author of this whole "authorship") I advance to meet the future. What may betide me in the immediate future I know not; how it will be in the following age when I have passed into history, that I know. But whatever it be that I know in this respect, it would be of no comfort to me, were I not in faith and confidence, though in humility and also in penitence, advancing to meet that future which is nearest of all and at every instant equally near—eternity.

—SOREN KIERKEGAARD, FROM *THE POINT OF VIEW*

Crossing the River

Colonel Campbell was a tall, strong retired army Colonel in his mid sixties. His examination at the military hospital revealed that he had bone cancer. He and his family had their usual time of devastation when that kind of news comes. As I visited with him and as he began to come to terms with his illness he said to me,

"I am not afraid to die, but I am just disappointed." He had so much to live for and had looked forward to a continuing productive and happy life. His expression of disappointment was a new one to me, but I immediately felt I understood. I realized I would feel that way if it happened to me.

Over a few months I visited with him. Usually I would read a few verses of Scripture and pray with him and his wife. One time I read from Isaiah 43:1, 2:

Fear not, for I have redeemed you;
 I have called you by name, you are mine.
 When you pass through the waters
 I will be with you;
 And through the rivers,
 They shall not overwhelm you.

Later as his illness was taking its toll and he was increasingly weak, after I visited and read a verse or two of scripture and prayed. As I started to leave his room he said, "Phil." I turned back to his bed and he said, "You have led me to the river's edge. Now how do I get across?" What a moment! I told him that in the book *Pilgrim's Progress*, Christian comes to the last river and was feeling overwhelmed by the waters, and his friend Hopeful said to him, "I feel the bottom, and it is good. Let your feet down on the solid rock of Christ." Christian did, and he walked through the waters of the river to the other side. I said put your whole trust in Jesus Christ, and he will carry you through. He nodded his understanding and acceptance. A few days later he crossed over the river to the other side.

My Boat

My boat is in the river of life.
In the trickling mountain stream
I put a small wood chip
And watch as it is carried along.
Sometimes it is barely moving,
And now and then it makes its way
Around a rock
Later to be detained in a side eddy,
Only again to be caught up
In the flowing stream
That ultimately leads to the sea.

So it is with my boat.
Sometimes it barely moves in still waters.
When the steam narrows it goes more quickly
And often makes its way around a rock
And is carried into a side eddy
Before it moves back into the stream
That winds its way through the turns and rapids
Moving along with the flow of time.
At last it is carried through
A deep and dark valley
Before it reaches the sea of God's eternity,

I believe: God was there at the beginning.
    God has been there all along.
    God will be there at the end.

JULY 7, 2009

Resurrection Miracle

Resurrection changes everything! It changes death into life, tragedy into triumph, the end into the beginning, despair into hope, defeat into victory, hate into love, brokenness into wholeness, darkness into light, time into eternity, bondage into freedom, and the old into the new. On and on one could go with the deep and dramatic changes which the fact of resurrection brings.

Enter into the miracle of resurrection this resurrection day! See everything in terms of life! Look again at everything in terms of possible transformation and a new dimension. Resurrection breaks the spell of death, darkness, and despair and lets in life, light, and newness.

Enter into the reality of this resurrection day! It means that we are alive forevermore. We shall have our incident of death, just as we have the incident of a night's sleep. But life is ours—eternal life. That is resurrection reality.

Enter into the joy and thrill of this resurrection day! Worship with expectancy! Sing open-heartedly! Be glad in the goodness and love of God! At any moment you may begin to live again with a new meaning, a new joy, and a new hope. Resurrection makes all the difference.

APRIL 7, 1966

Viewing Death from Jerusalem

We were on a family trip to the Holy Land. My brother William had been sick with cancer, but I did not know that death was near. We were staying in the King David Hotel in Jerusalem. My room overlooked the ancient walled city. About two in the morning I was awakened to a message that my brother William had died. For a couple of hours I tried to work out an airplane schedule to return to America. There was no way I could get it worked out. Finally resigning myself to the fact that I could not get to the States, I sat the remainder of the night looking out of the window to the night lighted ancient walled city of Jerusalem. There was where Jesus met his death by the horrible crucifixion. There was also the place where he had risen from the dead. For several hours I looked and thought. From the darkness there gradually came the dawn and the rising of the sun. I can never forget the rising of the sun over ancient Jerusalem and the awareness that the resurrection of Jesus Christ was real and that because he rose from the dead, we too shall live again, and that included my brother.

Graveside Talk

1st Soldier: What happened?
2nd Soldier: He arose!

1st :   He what?
2nd: He came back to life.

1st: How could he? People don't do that!
2nd: I don't know how. I only know he did.

1st: How do you know he did?
2nd: How do I know you are standing there?

1st: Do you think anybody will believe it?
2nd: I don't know.

1st: Do you think it will make any difference to people?
2nd: I don't know, but it makes a difference to me.

1st: Who is he anyway?
2nd: Some say he is God.

1st: Can God die?
2nd: I don't know, but he is alive now. I saw him.

1st: Fantastic! What if it is true?
2nd: It is true. You were here. How did you miss seeing him?

APRIL 2, 1970

Dear Thomas,

It is true beyond a shadow of a doubt! You ought to have been here! The other ten (pathetic Judas) of us were here and He was with us!

I know your reluctance to believe it. But He was unmistakable. His voice, his manner—and He showed his hands and side! I know you have said unless you *touch*, you will not believe. He was so real it just never occurred to try to touch him to prove him.

Thomas, I can't convince you and I shall not try. But you will know—if you do not stay apart from us. Too much is at stake (for you, that is) not to gather with us.

We do not know where all this will lead yet, but we do know that it is for real, and nothing will be the same again! You are one of us and we do not want you to miss it!

With new excitement, I am
Your friend and brother
Peter
(He calls me "Peter" in a way
nobody else does, and He
did it again.)

(Written on the Second Day of the Week)

Thank You, God, For This Day

To all who struggle and seek,
To all who suffer and hurt,
To all who face sickness and death,
To all who know sorrow and loss,

Listen with faith and you will hear
    The sounds of resurrection.
Look with faith and you will see
    The evidence of resurrection.
Believe and you will experience
    The miracle of resurrection.

The disciples say, "He is risen."
The angels say, "He is risen."
God has said, "He is risen."
Jesus has said, "Because I live
    You too shall live."

Thanks be to God!
    Alleluia!   Hallelujah!

APRIL 3, 1969

Graceful Aging

When John Quincy Adams was eighty years old,
a friend said to him, "Well, how is John Quincy
Adams?"

"Thank you," he responded. "John Quincy Adams
is quite well. But the house where he lives is
becoming dilapidated. It is tottering. Time and
seasons have nearly destroyed it, and it is becoming
quite uninhabitable. I shall have to move out soon.
But John Quincy Adams is quite well, thank you."

Walking in the Cemetery

I went to the cemetery today.
Beyond each monument there is a story
Of an earthly life that has ended.
What would their voices say
If they could speak now?
We do not know what each individual would say,
But their monuments with birth and death dates
May lead us to refocus our lives.
We can see the monument with our names
And birth date that we know so well,
And with the death date waiting to be chiseled there.
We know it is absolutely sure that time will come.

As I left the grave sites
And walked down two steps
There was a penny lying there.
Did it slip from the hand
Of one trying to take it with them?
Did he or she leave their last penny
As they entered the cemetery?
No. This did not literally happen,
But there is truth in this last penny.
Its truth causes me to refocus my life.

I did not see hates, ambitions, dreams, and regrets
Lying around on the ground,
Nor did I see the remains of
"I wish I had done this,"
Or "I wish I had not done that."
But there were many of these invisible
Things that were there.

As I leave the cemetery,
 I know there are some things
 I need to do before I come here
      To stay.

JANUARY 19, 2013

Part 13

God's Will

Tragedy: The Will of God?

I had to go to visit a mother who had lost a daughter in the most tragic circumstances. The death of the daughter had taken place as the result of an accident which was in any ordinary way impossible. To this day no one knows just how this accident happened, yet happen it did.

Now, when the accident was being investigated, a certain phrase was used by one of the chief investigators, a man with a long experience in such investigations. He said that the accident was so impossible that all that could be said was that it was "an act of God."

It is difficult to imagine a more terrible and a more blasphemous phrase. What kind of God can people believe in when they attribute the accidental death of a girl of twenty-four years of age to an act of God? How can anyone who is left possibly pray to a God who would do a thing like that?

During my own parish ministry I was never able to go into a house where there had been an untimely and tragic death or sorrow and say, "It is the will of God." When a child or a young person dies too soon, when there is a fatal accident, maybe due to someone's mistake or misjudgment, that is not "an act of God." Neither is it the will of God. It is in fact, the precise opposite of the will of God. It is against the will of God, and God is just as grieved about it as we are.

If a terrible and incurable disease strikes someone, if a child is run down and killed by a motor car, driven it may be by a reckless or drunken driver, if there is a disaster in the air or at sea or on the railway or on the roads, that is not the will of God. It is exactly and precisely what God did not will. It is due not to God's will, but to some human failure or to some human mistake.

God gave men free will because there could neither be goodness nor love without free will and exactly for that reason the action of men can run right counter to the will of God.

I do not think anyone can calculate the vast amount of damage that has been done by suggesting that terrible and tragic events in life are the will of God.

—WILLIAM BARCLAY

What Can Be Said When Tragedy Strikes?

When Jesus was on earth in the body, he healed the sick; he raised to life the little daughter of Jarius and the son of the widow at Nain. Quite clearly, Jesus did not think sickness and illness and untimely death the will of God. Quite clearly, he thought them the reverse of the will of God. They were the very things that he had come to help and to overcome. What, then can we say at a time like that?

We can say that God is as grieved as we are, that he is sharing in our sorrow and grief, that he is afflicted in all our afflictions, that his heart is going out to meet our heart.

We can say that he has it in his power to make it up to those who are taken too soon away, and to those to whom sorrow and suffering has tragically come. If God is justice and if God is love, I am as certain as it is possible to be certain of anything that there is a life to come. And in that life to come God is seeing to it that the life cut off too soon is getting its chance to blossom and flourish and the life involved in tragedy is finding its compensation. The eternal world is redressing the balance of the world of time.

We can say that Christianity has never pretended to explain sorrow and suffering. It may often be that in any tragedy there is traceable an element of human fault, human mistake, human sin; in any disaster the reason will lie in human error. Yet even when all such cases are taken into account there remains much that is simply inexplicable.

Christianity offers no cheap and facile explanation. In face of such things we often have to say, "I do not know why this happened." But what Christianity does triumphantly offer is the power to face these things, to bear them, to come through them on your own two feet, and even to transform them so that the tragedy becomes a crown.

—WILLIAM BARCLAY

When Tragedy Comes

When a father received word that his son had been killed
in a railroad accident, he turned to his pastor and cried
in desperation, "Tell me, sir, where was God when my
son was killed? Why didn't He prevent it?"

And in that tense and terrible moment divine guidance
was given to the minister. "My friend," he replied,
 "God was just where He was when
 His own Son was Killed!"

War and God's Will

Two sentries on the Jerusalem wall are discussing, why war? Second Sentry: Why does God hurl the nations against one another? There is room for all beneath the skies. There is still plenty of land unploughed; many forests still wait the axe. Yet men turn their ploughshares into swords, and hew living flesh with their axes. I cannot understand, I cannot understand. First Sentry: It has always been so.

Second Sentry: But must it always be so? Why does God wish the nations to fight?

First Sentry: The nations want war for its own sake.

Second Sentry: What are nations? Are not you one of our nation, am not I another? Are not our wives, your wife and mine, part of this same people? Did any of us want war? I stand here armed with a spear, not knowing against whom it is to be turned. Down there in the darkness, unwitting, waits the man for whom it is destined. I know him not, have never seen his face, or the breast I must pierce with death. In the enemy's camp another perchance warms his hands at the camp fire, the man who is to kill the father of my children. He has never seen me, and I have never done him harm. We are strangers, like trees in the forest. They grow quietly and bear their blossoms. But we rage furiously one against the other with axe and with spear, until our blood runs like resin, and therewith the life oozes forth. What puts death between the nations? What is it which sows hatred when there is room and to spare for life, and when there is abundant scope for love? I cannot understand, I cannot understand!

First Sentry: These things must be God's will, for they have always happened. I question no further.

Second Sentry: This crime cannot be God's will. He has given us our lives that we may live them. Everything that men do not understand they describe as God's will. War does not come from God. Whence comes it then?

First Sentry: How can I tell whence it comes? I know that there is war, and that it is useless to chatter about it. So do my duty; sharpen my spear, not my tongue.

—Stefan Zweig, *Jeremiah,*
a drama written during World War I

Part 14

Mystery

Needed Perspective

William Beebe, the naturalist, tells us of a ritual through which he and the late Theodore Roosevelt used to go at Aagamore Hill. "After an evening talk, perhaps about the fringes of knowledge, or some new possibility of climbing into the minds or senses of animals, we would go out on the lawn, where we took turns in an amusing little astronomical rite. We searched until we found, with or without glasses, the faint heavenly spot of light-mist beyond the lower left-hand corner of the great square of Pegasus, when one or the other of us would recite:

>   That is the Spiral Galaxy of Andromeda.
>   It is as large as our milky way.
>   It is one of a hundred million galaxies.
>   It is seven hundred and fifty thousand light-years away.
>   It consists of one hundred billion suns, each larger
>   than our sun.

After an interval, Colonel Roosevelt would grin at me, and say:

>   'Now I think we are small enough! Let's go to bed!'"

—WILLIAM SLOANE COFFIN

Mystery, Without and Within

I watch the vastness of the universe on television.
I see the wonders of the farthest reaches of knowledge
About the universe and how it functions.
The exploits of science and astronomy
Fill me with amazement
And stir my imagination about what is beyond
All the searching and probing of scientists and philosophers.

I know the earth is a planet
That turns on its axis
As it circles the sun,
But to envision it set in the expanse
Of the universe is to magnify
The mystery of it all.

And in the mystery of all we see,
And the unseen, unknown, and unimaginable beyond,
There is God!

And I? Just a speck
Smaller than a particle of dust
In a huge windstorm!
But this small bit of dust
Has been touched into life by God,
With a consciousness of being;
And with it, the mystery deepens.

OCTOBER 29, 2007

I Do Not Understand

There is so much that I do not understand.
In the world of nature:
    Ants come afar to a crumb.
    How do they know it is there?
    Spiders spin their intricate webs.
    How do they carry out its design?
    Mother birds sit on their eggs.
    How does the warmth bring forth a baby bird?
    And thousands of other wonders of nature happen every
day.
    Because I do not understand
    Does not negate the reality of it.

In the world of science:
    The vast universe is filled with floating stars and planets.
    How did all this come into being?
    Human voices are carried around the world on air waves.
    How can this happen?
    The magic of healing in the body and mind occurs,
    And occasionally medical science does not know how or why.
    And thousands of other wonders of science happen every day.
    Because I do not understand
    Does not negate the reality of it.

In the world of religion:
    God performs God's wonders in the world,
    And much of it is shrouded in mystery.
    The Spirit of God enters the human spirit
    And brings a transformation of life.
    Faith enables a person to endure trials and hardships
    And now and then brings a miracle.
    And thousands of other wonders of religion happen every day.

Because I do not understand
    Does not negate the reality of it.

Mystery

So, when I am told that the human spirit or soul
Moves from life on earth
To a state of eternal life,
Because I do not understand
Does not negate the reality of it.

AUGUST 15, 2005

The Silence of God

So it often is when God does not answer our prayers. Behind the silence are His higher thoughts. He is fitting stone to stone in His plan for the world and our lives, even though we can see only a confused and meaningless jumble of stones heaped together under a silent heaven. How many meaningless blows of fate there seem to be! –life, suffering, injustice, death, massacres, destruction; and all under a silent heaven which apparently has nothing to say. The cross was God's greatest silence. Then the power of darkness was allowed to make its final bid against the Son of God. Then the demons were unleashed and the most dreadful passions since the fall of Adam were given free rein. And God had nothing to say. There was simply the cry of the Dying asking of the silence why God had forsaken Him. God was silent even when dumb nature began to speak in an eloquent gesture and the sun withdrew its light. The stars cried out, and God was silent.

But now hear the great mystery of this silence. The very hour when God answered not a word or syllable was the hour of the great turning point when the veil of the temple was rent and God's heart was laid bare with all its wounds. Even when He was silent, God suffered with us. In His silence He experienced the fellowship of death and the depths with us. Even when we thought He did not care, or was dead, He knew all about us and behind the dark wings He did His work of love. We live in the power of this should we be without the knowledge that God sends his Son to us in the silent depths and valleys, that He is our Father in death; that He has indeed His high thoughts, that they come with power at Easter in glorious fulfillments surpassing all our expectations.

—HELMUT THIELICKE

The Guiding Light of Eternity

The night is dark and I am asleep.
Then comes the joyous light of day,
And I am awake.

But there is darkness within,
Until God gives the guiding light of eternity.
O God, while in the light of day
Illumine my darkness
With the guiding light of eternity.

(Thoughts stirred by an ancient Celtic invocation.)

OCTOBER 23, 2006

The Dawning

When I got up in the morning it was dark.
Then the dawn gradually came.
At first I could begin to see
The shapes and forms of trees,
Of buildings and then smaller objects.
There was the chirping of the birds
And I could see their colors,
Some brown, some blue, some red.
As the dawn turned to day
There was a whole world to see.

When I was born I was alive,
But so little I could see or know.
With a mother's love and care
And a father's watchful eye
I grew. I could see and feel.
In time I could sit up and walk.
As I heard words all around me
I began to jabber and then talk.
There was an ever expanding world
As I went from childhood to adulthood.

In early days there was spiritual darkness.
Then a spiritual dawn gradually came.
What was I? Who was I?
A human being with a body and a mind.
A mind that thought, wondered, and searched.
From it all emerged a human spirit.
The spirit reached out into the unknown.
What did it reach for? God?
Then inward light grew until
In Christ I could see the face of God.

SEPTEMBER 30, 2005

Mystery and Faith

There are mysteries that lie beyond our dust.
God's gift of the eye of faith
Enables us to trust God with those mysteries
When knowledge has no answers.

We seek to explore all mysteries,
And many past mysteries
Are mysteries no more.
But for all unexplainable mysteries,
And there will always be such mysteries,
The eye of faith
Will enable us to leave them
To the eternal God
Who moves in mysterious ways,
God's wonders to perform.

NOVEMBER 2, 2007

News from the Other Side of the Sky

The sky reaches from horizon to horizon.
And under its canopy is where
The hustle and bustle and struggle
Of human life takes place.
Eyes search under the bowl-like sky,
And the mind and spirit reach upward
With a yearning curiosity to know
What is on the other side of the sky.

Then on a quiet and still night,
A few unlettered shepherds
Were sleepily minding their flocks.
They were frightened by the silence
Being broken by a voice
That had never been heard before.
It reverberated deep in their frightened spirits.
Looking upward they saw no one,
But they heard the singing voices of an angel choir.
They were singing the Gloria.
The spoken voice and the sound of singing
Did not come from the hills and valleys
Where the sheep were grazing.
It came from the other side of the sky.
It brought wonderful and mysterious news.
When all was quiet again the shepherds wondered.
With wisdom not learned from philosophers' books,
But with the practical wisdom of simple shepherds
Who know well the ways of sheep,
With one accord, they said, "Let us go and see."

Thus the news from the other side of the sky
Was the good news that God cared
About the humans on planet earth
And had sent a Savior to bring

Mystery

A "Christmas Gift" of love.
That news, first given to lowly shepherds,
Is announced anew to every generation.
Now it is old good news announced again and again,
And those who receive it with faith
Not only know the wonderful love of God
But also peace and joy, more gifts of God.

(AT THE COMING OF DAWN, NOVEMBER 24, 2010)

God's Gift

Our mortal years
Are filled with labors and joys,
But also with struggles and sorrows.
God's gift is a deep sense
Of the mysteries that lie beyond our dust,
And an eye of faith
That looks beyond the visible horizon.

(Thoughts stirred by a prayer by Rufus Ellis)

NOVEMBER 2, 2006

Two Things

Two things fill the mind with ever new and increasing admiration and awe, the oftener and more steadily we reflect on them: the starry heavens above me and the moral law within me.

—IMMANUEL KANT

The Starry Heavens and the Soul

As a child I stretched out on the green grass,
Hands clasped behind my head.
I looked up at the blue sky
And wondered what was out there beyond the blue.
I also wondered what my future would be like.

Now at age ninety I sit in a chair,
Clasp my hands behind my head,
And look out at the blue sky
And wonder what is out there.
I also wonder what my future will be like.

Out there. We see the sun and the moon
And the planets and the vast milky way.
We think it is made up of millions
Of universes, some much larger than ours.
And we wonder what is beyond the milky way.
Is it a vast emptiness?
Or is it filled with unimaginable heavenly bodies?
And what is beyond them?
Do we ever get to absolute nothingness?
And how did all the starry heavens come to be?
Was the eternal God alone in a sea of nothingness,
And did God say: "I am going to bring into exisistence
All the starry heavens?"
Mystery. Deep mystery.
Mystery that fills us with wonder and awe.

And me. I look within, deep within,
And wonder what I am.
A body with a brain and an intricate system
That enables me to think, imagine, feel, love,
Cry, laugh, and worship.
I am more than body. I am a soul.

Mystery

When the body is no more,
My soul that has no physical elements
Is spirit as God is spirit.
The experience of my soul beyond death
Is a mystery. Deep mystery.

The starry heavens above and the soul within,
Both are filled with unfathomable mystery.
But the soul, which is you and me
Will be as the Father God has planned for us.

And All Will Be Well.

MARCH 2012

An Ineffable Mystery

He comes to us as one unknown, without a name, as of old, by the lake-side; He came to those men who knew Him not. He speaks to us the same words: "Follow thou me!" and sets us to the tasks which He has to fulfill for our time. He commands. And to those who obey Him, whether they be wise or simple, He will reveal Himself in the toils, the conflicts, the sufferings which they shall pass through in His fellowship, and, as an ineffable mystery, they shall learn in their own experience who He is.

—Albert Schweitzer
(E. N. Mosley's *The Theology of Albert Schweitzer*)

The Unseen Spirit of God

The ancient seer said to his son:
See the lump of clay,
See the bar of iron,
See the coin of silver.
They are what they are,
Solid and visible to the eye.

See the ounce of salt.
Put it in a glass of water tonight
And bring it to me tomorrow.
Tomorrow comes. Bring the salt.
Can you see the salt, my Son?
I see only water, no salt.
Sip the water, my son.
It tastes salty.

In the same way, my Son,
You cannot see the Spirit of God,
But in truth, God is here.

NOVEMBER 14, 2006

Unseen But Real

From a small grain of corn
Comes a beautiful green stalk
With a yellowish tassel on top.
Can you break into the grain
And see the essence
That brings forth the living stalk?
There is nothing identifiable
As life that can be seen.
Crush it into pieces and the result is cornmeal.
Place the cornmeal in the ground
And nothing will grow from it.
Put a whole grain in the ground
And from it will grow the stalk.
When we cracked the corn
We could not see or find life,
But it was there somewhere
Totally unseen within the grain.
Mystery.

There are many things invisible
But that are real
And work in mysterious ways.
In our lives we must make room
For invisible realities, such as God,
To work in marvelous ways.
Mystery.

NOVEMBER 14, 2006

The Mystery and Wonder of Life

The throbbing of life is felt on the farm.
The spirited horse, the stolid mule,
The contended cow chewing its cud,
The wallowing pig, the barking dog,
The crowing rooster, the cackling hens,
The soft and fragile newly hatched chicks,
The singing birds, the frisky squirrels,
And hundreds of other forms of life.

Then there are the humans,
Surveying all the life around,
With their special gifts of thinking,
Imagination, emotions, laughing, and crying,
And abilities far superior
As we are made in the image of God.

But in all life there is the strong will to live.
Each living being has its place
In the grand structure of the created world.
Sometimes the mystery and wonder of life
Breaks through our daily routine
Of coming and going, getting and spending,
And in that feeling of mystery and wonder
There emerges the gentle but strong
Reverence for life—our lives,
And life in all its forms.
And a depth within is touched.

(Thoughts stirred by Albert Schweitzer's ethic of the Reverence for Life.)

NOVEMBER 1, 2006

Thoughts on the Beginning

Astronomy fascinates me.
Present day scientific exploration
Of moon and planets
Stretches my mind and inflames my imagination.

The moon has been a romantic body in the sky.
But now we know it is a large ball
Of rock and rock-like substances.
We have set foot on the moon.
Now there are plans to plant a colony there!
From there we can better explore planets
And other bodies in space.
The mass of material that is the moon—-
Where did it come from?
It came from the action and interaction
Of other elements in space.
But where did those elements come from?
And where did the elements that
Produced those elements come from?

Going back and back with that question
We probe beyond the billions and billions of years
Wondering if there ever was a time
When there were no substances out there!
We go back trillions and trillions of years
And at some point we reach the beginning,
When there was nothing. That is,
Unless the substances of the earth, moon, and stars
Are eternal, that is, have always been.
If in the probing and stretching of our minds
We do reach the beginning of it all,
Then, how did it begin?

Mystery

God only is eternal, no beginning and no end.
So God created the earth and heavens
Out of nothing!
That is the God, clothed in mystery,
Whom we worship.

NOVEMBER 5, 2007

The Infinite One

Where did it all come from?
The earth, the sun, the moon,
And the millions of galaxies
That fill the sky on a starry night,
And the unseen and unknown universes
That fill the infinite space.
Unless the atoms that make up
The substances of the planets and stars
Are eternal, then someone or something
Had to bring it into being from nothing.

Deep within human beings, ancient and modern,
Is a sense of *one*
Who brought it into being,
And who is still active in the present.

The concepts of this *one*
Who was before anything existed
Are varied and imperfect.
The Christian believes that the "I am"
Became incarnate in Jesus Christ,
And through him we have a clearer understanding
Of the nature of the great "*I am*."
In Christ the nature of the *one*
Is revealed as a heart of love
For all of creation,
Including the human being.

So, as we live, think, and feel
In the midst of the complexities of life,
We can sense that
"The heart of the infinite is wonderfully kind."

NOVEMBER 7, 2007

God's Image

God said, "Let us make man in our image."
Genesis 1:26

So, we are made in God's image!
We are created body, mind, and soul (spirit).
The three are not separate, but one.
We are certainly not God or Gods,
But we are made to "look like God."
A portrait is an image of a person,
But it is a likeness, not the being that is.

So, if we are made in the image of God,
How do we look like God?
Certainly not in our fleshly bodies.
In our minds?
"We have the mind of Christ,"
So the apostle Paul writes about Christians.
We "image" Christ
When we think like him,
And Christ was the image of the invisible God.
In our spirits?
We "image" God when we have the spirit of Christ,
Because the spirit of Christ was the spirit of God.
So, when we look at a person,
Do we see an image of God?
We do not see that image in the physical body,
But we may see a partial image of God
When we know the person's mind and spirit.
We say "may" see an image of God
Because we may not see God's image.
There are minds and spirits which
Do not reflect what God is like.
Is it not true that in some minds and spirits
We can image the evil one?

When that is the case
We, with our human freedom,
Have turned the image of God
In which we were created
Into an image of the evil one.
That image does not give
Us a picture of what God is like.

Can we completely eradicate the
Image of God within us?
Maybe so. Maybe not.

OCTOBER 17, 2007

God Has Endowed Our Nature

God has endowed our nature
With a wonderful quality.
We can apprehend the Divine because
God imprinted on our heart
The likeness of his own nature.

But in the process of living
There has been poured all around
The heart, a wax
Which when hardened has obscured
The wonderful quality
That was given in childhood.

If this plaster like wax
Can be broken off the heart
Or melted or washed away,
The divine beauty of the heart
Will shine again as it did
When we were first made
In the image of God.

(Thoughts from readings of Gregory of Nyssa)

JULY 18, 2006

The Stars Are There

The stars fill the sky
And sparkle with their beauty
When night has settled over the earth.

Sometimes drifting clouds
Obscure the stars until they pass,
And only now and then do we see the stars.
Sometimes the dark clouds are heavy
And fill the sky from horizon to horizon,
And there is no glimmer of the stars.
   But they are there.

We live our lives beneath the stars
That bless us with their beauty,
And in the mystery of the universe
They fill us with wonder
And a sense of the infinite God
As well as a sense of our own finiteness.

Then some cloud drifts into our lives
And for a while we do not see the stars of God.
Sometimes the clouds are heavy and dark
And hang over our lives from horizon to horizon,
And there is not a glimmer of the stars.
   But the stars are there.

We have seen the stars
And we know they are there.
God's gift of faith sustains us
Until the dark clouds are gone
And we can see the stars again.

(Thoughts stirred by the poem "Faith," by G. A. Studdert Kennedy)

NOVEMBER 12, 2006

The Upward Reach

"Thou hast put an upward reach
Into the heart of man." *

The upward reach is there
Buried in the complexity of the human being.
And sometimes it does seem to be buried,
Covered over by the heavy soil
Of selfishness, greed, and sensuality.

In the early days of spring, the crocus
Pushes its way through the soil and blooms.
The seed of eternity is in the heart of man,
And as the seasons of life come and go,
The upward reach will emerge.

*From *God the Architect* by Harry Kemp

FEBRUARY 10, 2006

An Important Thing to Know

The important thing is to know our purpose in entering the inner world, and to know that we are looking for the Risen Christ and a relationship with Him."

—MORTON T. KELSEY

Spirit to Spirit

We are more than a physical body.
There is the wonderful intangible
That is the soul or spirit or psyche.
It is mysteriously interwoven with the body,
But when the body becomes still and lifeless
This intangible continues to be.

The Word became incarnate in human flesh.
God's intangible Spirit became interwoven with the body.
When the body of Jesus was crucified
It became still and lifeless.
God in Jesus did not cease to be.
But in the mystery beyond comprehension and understanding
It manifested itself again in the Risen Christ.

As we in our living bodies reach beyond them
To the intangible part of us
Which is soul, spirit, or psyche,
We probe in the world of spirit.
And that is the world of the Risen Christ.
There with spirit to spirit
A spiritual relationship can occur.
When it does and the relationship grows,
We then experience the transforming
Power of the spirit of Christ.
Living in that relationship we experience
Deep and significant changes taking place in us.
And bit by bit a new, stronger, and better person emerges.

JULY 27, 2006

The Life-Giving Stream of God's Love

The mountains stand solid and rugged
And loom up against the sky.
Their crags seem impenetrable
And hikers find them formidable.
But walking along the side of the stream
Which flows down the mountain side
And through the valleys
Is pleasant and delightful
And is done with relative ease.
It brings a quietness and peace to the human spirit.

The great imponderables of life,
And the answers to the heaviest questions
That philosophers and religionists
Have sought in vain,
Have stood silhouetted like the mountains
Against the eternal sky of God.
But the unknowing and humble person
With God's gift of faith
May walk along the stream
Of God's eternal love
That flows through the hard imponderables
And mysteries of the universe and life,
And in the wonder of God's love
Find an assurance that brings quietness and peace.

(Thoughts stirred by reading from Albert Schweitzer,
The Nature of Christianity)

NOVEMBER 2, 2006

The Great Artist

I saw God paint the sky this morning,
On a broad canvas of dark blue.
God painted with colors of pale rose
And yellow hues that blended into gold.
Moving toward the top of the canvas
God painted over the dark blue
With light blue, splotched here and there
With billowy white.

Then God laid down the brushes
To go about the day's work.
God's task is to oversee
The work of millions and millions of laborers,
Working in thousands upon thousands of places,
Spread out on seven continents
And upon the earth's restless seas.

So vast is God's memory
That God can call the names of every laborer,
And God knows the name of every spouse and child.
So sensitive is God's hearing
That God hears every baby's cry,
And the heavy breathing of the dying.
So keen is God's sight that God sees
What each one is doing.
So deep is God's love that every hurt is felt,
And every joy is celebrated.

Then the quiet of the evening comes,
And God picks up his brushes again.
God dips the brush in pots of red.
And on the darkening canvas
Pale red turns into darker hues of red,
And the huge orange ball

Begins to disappear over the edge.
God's final touch is to cast a handful of stars
Onto the darkened canvas,
And they become points of light for the night.
And the day that God has made gently closes
As the quiet hush of evening comes.

There will be many more tomorrows,
And God will lovingly create each one
And graciously offer them as a gift to God's people.

KIAWAH ISLAND, JANUARY 4, 2004

In Church

We had church yesterday.
People came and sat in pews.
They stood to sing the hymns.
They bowed their heads to pray.
An anthem was sung.
A sermon was preached.
The benediction was pronounced.
And the people went out.

In the mystery of worship,
  What happened?
  God knows.

MAY 26, 1958

Musings Sitting on a Seminary Bench

I muse as I sit on a Seminary bench,
Seeing lush green grass, and rich green trees
Against a beautiful Wedgewood blue sky.

The planet earth, is a ball circling and spinning in space.
Time was when the earth was covered
with the undisturbed growth of flora and fauna,
the blue waters of oceans, the clear mountain streams,
and thunderous waterfalls, and capped with white snow
at both the North and South poles.

What if something, like a meteor of enormous size
Struck the earth and moved it out of its orbit,
And it would go spinning out of control!
Would it be fire or ice?
Or it stays in its present orbit,
Just the right distance from the sun.

Over millions and millions of years,
The earth has changed.
And beings on the earth have changed.
The dinosaurs have come and gone.
I wonder how many other living beings
Were on the earth and now are gone.

Then millions of years ago man came
To this virgin and unbelievable beautiful earth.
For millions of years now the human being
Has populated the earth.
Man stands as the most intelligent being
On earth at the highest pinnacle of God's creation.

Man's intelligence, imagination, and skill
Has gradually changed the planet earth.

Mystery

There are ribbons of concrete on every continent.
There are cities that send skyscrapers into the sky.
There are scars on the surface of the earth,
Put there by the mining for minerals.
Holes are bored into the earth
Bringing forth billions and billions of
Gallons of oil and gas, leaving massive empty spaces.
Ravaging of the trees of the forests have left bald spots.

I wonder if in millions of years,
The man made and natural changes
On the planet earth, will result
In the extinction of mankind,
As the changes in earlier millions of years
Resulted in the extinction of dinosaurs.
And if mankind disappears I wonder
What living beings on earth will emerge?
And populate the planet earth.

Just thinking and wondering!

SEPTEMBER 8, 2010

Part 15

Atheism

Atheism

I know all the difficulties which confront theism—especially the problem of evil— but I am sure that Professor William Montague was right when he said that the chance of atheistic materialism's being true would have to be represented by a fraction, with one for the numerator and a denominator that would reach from here to the fixed stars.

—HARRY EMERSON FOSDICK

Is Atheism Possible

Genuine atheism is not humanly possible.

PAUL TILLICH

College Atheist

You are not the first college student to give up religion. Here is a youth who called himself an atheist. He rebelled against his inherited religion so vehemently that once when his family took him to church he made a disturbance and was publicly rebuked. Who was that youth? You never would guess, unless by chance you knew. That was Robert Browning who afterward wrote:

I say, the acknowledgement of God in Christ,
    Accepted by reason, solves for thee
    All questions in the earth and out of it.

Yes, *that* Robert Browning.

So, I am hoping that you too will come through to a faith that will alike create and sustain the goodness you dream of.

—HARRY EMERSON FOSDICK

Natural Revelation

As the perfection of a happy life consists in the knowledge of God, that no man might be precluded from attaining felicity, God hath not only sown in the minds of men the seed of religion, already mentioned, but hath manifested himself in the formation of every part of the world, and daily presents himself to public view, in such a manner, that they cannot open their eyes without being constrained to behold him. His essence indeed is incomprehensible, so that his majesty is not to be perceived by the human senses; but on all his works he hath inscribed his glory in characters so clear, unequivocal, and striking, that the most illiterate and stupid cannot exculpate themselves by the plea of ignorance.

—JOHN CALVIN

Many Call It God

In his agony Byrd considered sleeping pills, but instead wrote in his diary:

The universe is not dead. Therefore, there is an Intelligence there, and it is all pervading. At least on purpose, possibly the major purpose, of that Intelligence is the achievement of universal harmony.

Striving in the right direction for Peace (Harmony), therefore, as well as the achievement of it, is the result of accord with that Intelligence.

It is desirable to effect that accord.

The human race, then, is not alone in the universe. Though I am cut off from human beings, I am not alone.

For untold ages man has felt an awareness of that Intelligence. Belief in it is the one point where all religions agree. It has been called by many names. Many call it God.

—ADMIRAL BYRD

Part 16

General

Once There Was a Planet Called Earth

Once there was a planet called earth.
It was full of life, many forms of life,
On the land, in the sea, and in the sky.
It was covered with luscious green trees and plants.
The ocean waters were blue as the sky.
The North and South poles were capped with white.
And the earth circled the sun
And the moon circled the earth.
It was the most beautiful planet
In the solar system.
And above all it was a wonderful home
For the human race for millions of years.

Now it is dead.
It still circles the sun,
But there is no life on it.
No beautiful green of living trees and plants.
No marine life in the oceans.
And no human life.
What happened?
It is a horrifying nightmare.
We hope, pray, and work
That the nightmare will never become a reality.

APRIL 3, 2009

When Tyrants Are Afraid

In Robert Browning's poem "Instans Tyrannus," which means
"the threatened tyrant," he describes in monologue, with the
tyrant speaking, the various punishments he inflicted on the
poor victims.
Then when the tyrant has done his worst,
he discovers the truth that the
weakest man with God is stronger
that the strongest man without God.

I

Of the millions or two, more or less,
I rule and possess,
One man, for some cause undefined,
Was least to my mind.

II

I struck him, he groveled of course
For what was his force?
I pinned him to earth with my weight
And persistence of hate:
And he lay, would not moan, would not curse,
As his lot may be worse.

VII

When sudden . . . how think ye, the end?
Did I say "without friend"?
Say rather, from marge to blue marge
The whole sky grew his targe

With the sun's self for visible boss,
Whani and Arm ran across
Which the earth heaved beneath like a breast
Where the wretch was safe prest!
Do you see? Just my vengeance complete,
The man sprang to his feet,
Stood erect, caught at God's skirts, and
    Prayed!
So, I was afraid!

—ROBERT BROWNING

To Graduating Friends

You did not ask to be born.
Neither did we.
You inherit a world you did not make.
So did we.
You do not like many things as they are.
Neither do we.

We tried to affect the world in our generation.
Some of us are still trying.
You want to affect the world in your generation?
Great! Only fools deny it needs changing.

Don't despair!
And let your youth keep us from despairing.
Keep on, until your own child's youth
Keeps you from despairing.

Two thoughts.
There are a host of older friends pulling for you,
And some working with you,
Who have neither chosen selfish ease
Nor have drowned in cynical pessimism.
The other thought: Long before either of us
Arrived on earth and in time,
There was "The One" at work.
Are you surprised that that One is not
Satisfied with it either?

The three of us together
Can do more than either one alone.

MAY 20, 1971

Little Things of Childhood

We lived in the country.
No electricity. No running water.
Fireplaces and a well.
How old was I?
Three, four, five or six?

Winter mornings were cold.
When my eyes popped open
I threw back the covers
And ran to Papa's room
To the fire in the fireplace.
The wood was blazing and crackling
As it pushed back the cold.
When one side warmed
I turned the other side
Until it felt good all over.

On the hearth beside the fire
Was the poker. Not just a poker,
But *the* poker.
It was solid iron, long and straight
With a loop at the top
And a hook at the other end.
The poker was to poke the fire,
And then the blaze would get bigger
And the sparks would fly up
As they made the crackling noise.

How wonderful I thought it was!
Gazing into the fire
My childish mind wondered:
When I grow up will I have
A wonderful poker like this?
Now in the cold winter time,
The octogenarian that I am,
I sit by the fire

And occasionally poke it with a
Solid iron, long and straight poker
With a loop at the top
And a hook at the other end,
And watch the fire blaze
And hear the crackle of the sparks, And my heart is filled
And runs over with gratitude.

NOVEMBER 3, 2005

Now That I Am Fourscore and Retired

Now that I am retired:
I do not have work imposed schedules;
No required meetings to attend;
No congregation expecting a sermon.
There is a welcomed freedom,
And there is unhurried time.
It is still filled with many things,
But most of all my spirit
Reaches both without and within.

I revel in the wonders of nature.
I value the warmth of human love.
I reflect with deep gratitude
On the loving providence of God.
I feel the soothing strokes of peace.
I am awakened at the light
Of each new day; my spirit throbs.
I gratefully accept God's gift of faith,
And with millions who have gone before me,
I face the future with quiet confidence
And inward assurance that the steadfast love of God
Endures forever, even from everlasting to everlasting.

FEBRUARY 26, 2006

Simeons and Annas

Simeon and Anna were old.
Anna was eighty-four
And probably wished her age had not been told.
Simeon was old, but no age was given,
Even though he would not have cared.
They both looked for the longed for Kingdom
That had not come.
But they did not give up hope.

They cradled a child in their arms,
And their faces brightened, and their eyes lit up,
As faith and hope warmed their hearts.
The Kingdom would come!
This child of God would bring it in.
Their tenacious faith and quiet assurance
Stirred hope in younger minds and hearts
Who wondered if they could believe
That God's Kingdom would come.

Today, we are God's older servants.
Some of our ages are known, others not.
We have cradled a grandchild
In the crook of our arm,
And looked into a little face
With tender love and strong hope,
A new life with all its possibilities,
And in joy and fear and hope, we breathed a prayer.

At Christmas time the Simeons and Annas
Symbolically hold the Christ child in their arms,
And with joy and fear and hope affirm:
The Kingdom will come!
The younger generation will see,
And they too will have their hearts

Stirred with faith and hope, and say:
Yes. The Kingdom will come!
Thus hope is passed from generation to generation.

SEPTEMBER 25, 2002

Drinking Poison Out of a Golden Cup

Drinking poison out of a golden cup!
What a striking phrase!
It is a metaphor of those
Who have great wealth—everything,
But who are ruining their lives
By the way they are living them.
The news these days is full
Of celebrities who are doing just that.

But what kind of cup am I drinking from?
Not gold, but silver, crystal, pottery, plastic, or paper?
Before I am too quick to condemn
Those who are drinking poison out of a golden cup,
I need to ask myself, am I drinking poison
Out of my cup, whichever it is.

AUGUST 22, 2007

Beach Lesson

I took a folding chair and a book to the beach.
The book: *Tuesday with Morrie.*
It describes Morrie's death with Lou Gherig's disease.
This is not what it is about!
It is about lessons of life learned in dying.

I watched the waves gently lapping on the sandy beach
As the tide was coming in.
Each wave brought the water a few inches nearer to me.
An older couple walked by between the waves and me.
As he continued to walk he said, "You are gonna get your
    feet wet."
I replied, "You reckon so?"

I have a birthday coming soon.
Each birthday is a wave,
Bringing the ocean's edge a few inches closer.
I have been reading Morrie's book.

A hairy chested middle aged man walked by.
"Oh, I see you are reading Morrie's book.
I read it and really enjoyed it.
I bought four copies and gave it to friends.
I told them to pass it on."

We talked a bit.
He pointed out turtle's nests.
The female turtle crawls up the sandy beach,
Digs out a place in the sand,
And deposits about a hundred eggs.
She leaves them. In time they hatch.
After a while all the little hatched turtles
Will come back to this same place
And deposit their eggs.
This process will be repeated time and again.

Such are the wonders of the natural world
Of which we are a part.
We are born, live, and have our day.
Every wave of the incoming tide
Brings the water's edge a bit closer.
Ultimately it reaches us.

Such are the wonders of the natural world
Of which we are a part.
Can we see the hand of God
In the way of the turtle
And in the waves of the incoming tide?

JULY 13, 2000

A Special Moment at Christmas

Biblical insight from the ancient witness of Job tell us,
"Lo, these are but the outskirts of his ways,
And how small a whisper do we hear of him."
With the year of 2003 filled with "man's inhumanity to man,"
We often feel we only know the fringes of God's outskirts,
And God's whisper can hardly be heard.
Then in a quiet and still moment in the Christmas season,
There is a fleeting glimpse of swaddling clothes,
And a baby's soft cry is heard,
And somewhere deep in our hearts,
We sense that in spite of all,
    God is love!
And in that moment of faith, hope is ignited.

CHRISTMAS 2003

A Rock for the Centuries

First (Scots) Presbyterian Church is a rock for the centuries.
Twelve Scottish families had a vision:
A Church like their Church in Scotland!
Thus began First (Scots) long Scottish heritage.

The year was Seventeen hundred and Thirty One,
One year before George Washington was born,
Twelve years before Thomas Jefferson was born.
Twenty-four years before Alexander Hamilton was born,
Forty-five years before the Declaration of Independence.

First (Scots) has survived
    The American Revolution,
    The War Between the States,
    The Earthquake of 1886,
    World War I,
    World War II,
    The Church's fire in 1945,
    Hurricane Hugo in 1989,
The preaching of its 22 Senior Ministers since 1731! *

First (Scots) Presbyterian Church is a rock for the centuries.
In the beginning of the Twenty-first Century,
It is a strong, vital Church,
Throbbing with the heart-beat of the Gospel.
It is a solid rock for now and for centuries to come.

*Woodrow Wilson said the proof of the divinity of the gospel is that it has survived 2000 years of preaching. (His father was a Presbyterian Minister.)

—MINISTER EMERITUS

Written for the occasion of the 275th anniversary of First (Scots)
Presbyterian Church, Charleston, South Carolina, September 10, 2006

Thoughts on a Quadrangle Bench

Seminary is a special place,
    A very special place.

Who goes there?
    Seekers and becomers.
    The hungry and the thirsty.
    The inquirers and the yearners.

Who is there?
    Theologians and scholars.
    Teachers and interpreters.
    Preachers, pastors and prophets.

Who goes out from there?
    Servants
    Who carry the gifts of God,
    Who stand behind the sacred desk,
    Who offer a crust of bread and a cup of water,
    Who tell of forgiveness and a second chance,
    Who enter where tragedy has come,
    Who shine a ray of hope in the darkness,
    Who stoop to help pick up the pieces
    Of a broken home or shattered life,
    Who share the faith that penetrates
    The curtain of death.

What reward do we have?
    To hear the words of their Master,
    "Well done, good and faithful servant."
    That is enough.

SEPTEMBER 21, 2004

Prayer

Eternal God,
We worship you as the Lord of all that there is.
You are Creator, Sustainer, and Redeemer.
To you be the kingdom and the power and the glory
    forever and forever.

Set within a world that challenges us daily, we need
    the grace and strength that your constant presence
    can bring.

Give us faith that doubt cannot overshadow.
Give us hope that dissipates discouragement.
Give us love that is stronger than hate.
Give us trust that cannot be destroyed by cynicism.
Give us gentleness that rules out violence.
Give us courage that overcomes fear.
Give us your Spirit that we may not die spiritually.
Give us vision that we may not be without dreams.
Give us guidance that we may not lose our way.
Give us light that can never be put out by darkness.
Give us singleness of heart that we may not be pulled
    into pieces.
Give us purpose lest we lose the reason for living.

And if, O God, you choose to so bless us, give us
    one thing more: the desire and ability to use
the life you have given us to benefit others.

We pray in the name of the strong Son of God,
Jesus Christ, our Lord.
    Amen

(Prayer at the Church Pensions Conference
in New York City, December 1, 1988)

The Christmas Creche

As Christmas draws near
The Nativity crèche is carefully arranged
On a table to be the center
Of the Christmas decorations.
The manger goes in the center.
Then there is sweet Mary,
And the proud but humble Joseph,
Both near the manger.
The others pieces are carefully placed one by one.
There are a couple of sheep,
A donkey, a cow, and a camel.
There are two shepherds
And three wise men bearing gifts.
Then there is a different dimension added
As an angel and a star
From the outer world complete the scene.

Poor animals. Sheep, donkey, cow, and camel.
They do not know the wonder of the moment.
They have no capacity to understand.
The shepherds who have seen the angels
And heard their singing are puzzled.
The wise men are mystified
As they have followed a new star
In the western sky.
Mary and Joseph are relieved that the child is born.
They look around in the humble stable
And knowing that something special is happening
They ponder the deeper meaning of these events.

And we! The Christmas decorations
And other trappings of Christmas
Are to be completed.
The tree decorated, with ornaments and lights.

The wrapped gifts put under the tree.
A Christmas carol or the refrain of
I'm dreaming of a white Christmas
Stirs our imagination and we see
Snow covered trees and hear
The jingling of sleigh bells.

And finally Christmas Eve comes.
The children have reluctantly gone to bed.
The lights of the Christmas tree
Cast a glow, and the warming fire
Of the Christmas logs draws us
To sit quietly and let the hectic events
Of Christmas preparations settle down
And give way to a much needed
Gentle, quiet, and pensive feeling.

As we sit by the warming and flickering fire,
Perhaps we too ponder the events
Around the Savior's birth.
Though quietly given, the birth of Jesus
Was a pivotal point of human and divine history,
Which divided time into B.C. and A.D.
It was a silent cataclysmic event
That marked the beginning of changes
That would reverberate throughout the world.

The animals had no capacity to know.
The Shepherds knew something was happening
But did not comprehend its significance.
Joseph and Mary knew that somehow
God was in this event.

And we! In the quiet beauty and stillness of Christmas,
To us, maybe, just maybe, silently the wondrous gift is given,
And there opens up the vista
Of earthly life and the heavenly life of eternity.
As the birth of Jesus

Marked the dramatic beginning of a new world,
So this Christmas may mark a dramatic rebirth,
Or a rekindling of our human spirit—-and for us
A new world of joy and peace and love begins.
And once again we have experienced
The wonderful miracle of Christmas.

NOVEMBER 19, 2011

I wish I could give each of you a special gift during this Christmas Season. God has already given us a capacity which animals and other creatures do not have. That is the capacity to understand something of the wonderful miracle and mystery of Jesus' birth—God incarnate in human flesh. My gift to you would be the gift of a few golden moments of silence when your mind and spirit reach deep for the heart of the meaning of Christmas, and as you touch its reality, you will have an experience of inner peace and of rekindled faith and renewed hope as we live in a troubled and turbulent and uncertain world.